KEVIN WICZER

DIVINE

LESSONS

from YOUR

GUIDES

Published in the United States by GetKevInsight Press.

www.GetKevInsight.com

First Edition

ISBN: 979-8-9936551-0-9

Thank you to Armando, Mom and Dad, my family, my friends, my spirit guides, my higher self, and all of those who have been a part of my continuing journey. Sending you so much love!

ABOUT THE AUTHOR

What an amazing experience this spiritual journey continues to be!

In May of 2024 I began a personal soul search. I felt a bit lost inside, and I did not understand why. I was a theatre guy. I directed shows and was a playwright. I thought I had my life planned out. But suddenly theatre was becoming more of a battle with myself than it ever was and I didn't know why.

I felt like I had no special purpose even though I knew that art had the potential to heal. But it wasn't healing me. It was burdening me instead. It was not that I would never want to direct again, but it just wasn't filling my cup anymore. This was a hard pill to swallow because this was my life path, or so I thought. I began a deep dive to find myself and my soul's purpose.

Someone mentioned to me about life path numbers, and from finding my life path number (Master Life Path 11), I needed to know more about what that meant. I kept hearing that 11s are extremely intuitive and are also empaths, and I started listening to multiple mediums and psychics talking about the same things: that we are only here to love ourselves, spread love to others, learn and teach lessons, rediscover who we truly are, and raise the energy frequency of this planet. That spreading joy and helping and healing others would do just that.

I started watching spiritual podcasts and listening to all the messages of love. A message I heard time and time again was: if you completely open yourself to your spirit guides and Source (God), amazing things will start happening. So, one night, before I went to sleep, I laid in my bed and said that I would be completely open to helping and healing others in any way my spirit guides wanted me to.

The next morning, there was a very strange, unexplainable shift. I started getting soft messages, in my own voice, on the right side of my head. It would say "Help so and so" or "Contact this person." And when I did, I found I would start helping them with some kind of validation that they needed to hear and affirmations to guide them in the right direction. I didn't understand completely at first because I thought I might have been making it up in my mind. But somehow, I was able to help people and validate what they needed to hear to begin healing.

Then I was watching a spiritual podcast, and someone was showing their tarot cards and said that anyone can do it, and I paused the video as they put their deck in front of the camera. Immediately I heard, "Buy the deck." It was the Universal Rider-Waite-Smith deck, and after I bought it, along with the tarot guide, I learned all 78 cards in less than a couple weeks. I couldn't explain how I caught on so quickly, and that, mixed with my intuition, led me to reading the decks for myself. Then for my family.

Three tarot decks and five oracle decks later, I started reading for friends, and then people from all over the world. Helping and healing others through tarot and oracle cards was my *new* Life Path. Doors began opening to me in ways I never could have imagined. I had found myself.

Each lesson of the day came from my spirit guides who spoke to me through my tarot decks as well as information they put in my mind – channeling. I pulled two cards daily to create the lessons with my guides. I got the message to share these beautiful lessons. And so it is. In this book, one lesson may seem like another, but that is no coincidence. Each hold different messages and frequencies within them.

The fact that my guides' lessons have begun to help people, has validated that this is the path I must be on and continue. Sending love and light to you all!! Know that we're never alone! There are so many beautiful and incredible beings rooting for us!!

Trust the process and believe!

Visit: www.GetKevInsight.com

HOW TO USE THIS BOOK OF DIVINE LESSONS

This book of channeled lessons is your guide to help you when you feel stuck or need spiritual guidance. Within these pages you will feel the beautiful and powerful healing energy of the Divine.

There are a couple of ways to use this book. Do what feels right for you – there is no right or wrong way to use it – but here are a couple of suggestions from my guides:

The first way they suggest using this book is by reading a lesson every day, one by one. Each lesson will be able to give you wonderful and spiritual insight to help you on your journey through life. Every day, open to the next lesson and see what your guides have to offer you. The lessons are in no special order – they are in the order that my spirit guides told me to write them as I wrote them. Nothing has been moved or shifted. Journal about how you relate to each lesson as well if you wish.

The second way to use this book, and my spirit guides' and my favorite way, is by using this book like an oracle. Close your eyes and set an intention in your mind. Focus on the intention of what you really need to learn that day. With your eyes closed, flip through the book. Go back and forth from front to back and back to front, until you feel pulled to stop and look at the lesson that is written. The lesson will resonate with you either at that moment, or very soon after. Journaling how the lessons relate to your life is also beneficial.

If you use the second method, and you land on the same lesson more than once, take note that it is a very important lesson that your guides want you to learn. There are no coincidences, and everything happens for a reason. If you land on a lesson again and again, try to begin to understand the message your guides are trying to send to you. You can even put a little tally up in the corner of the page with pencil, to see how many times you have landed on that one lesson. Watch for patterns and take note.

Your guides also recommend journaling about the lesson daily. Write down how the lesson resonates with you in your life. What comes up in your mind that you need to address? Writing your thoughts down on paper or typing it out really helps with reflection. And self-reflection is so important for all of us so that we can continue to heal, learn, and grow.

Sending you all love and light as always!!

Happy Journeying!!!

Kevin Wiczer and the Guides

KEVIN WICZER

DIVINE

LESSONS

from YOUR

GUIDES

THE GIFT OF PEACE

Today's lesson of the day is that one of the best gifts we can give ourselves is the gift of peace. Know that everything works out the way it is supposed to for a certain reason. Most of the time they are lessons we need to learn. We do not have to understand it right away, but we need to be at peace within ourselves. We cannot control each other, and we certainly cannot control the world. But we can control our own peace within us. It is ours and cannot be taken away from us.

Tragedies always have and will continue in our lives. The questions the guides want you to ask yourself is: Why was I meant to go through it? And what can I learn from it? Why do we have to go through sickness or loss? We need to reflect on these things to then be at peace with them. And from that peace we can have understanding.

Take a moment to reflect on your past and present joys and tragedies and ask yourself why you needed to go through them and what lessons you needed to learn. The universe always and already has a plan for you, and you are exactly where you are supposed to be at this exact moment. Nothing is by chance or a mistake.

So, instead of living in fear, which is a very low energy vibration, live in peace, which is a high energy vibration. High energy frequencies will attract other high energy frequencies. Just know you are loved, and you are never alone. You always have a spirit team around you, rooting for you.

Sending love and light!!

NEGATIVE FREQUENCY

Today's lesson of the day is to understand that negativity of all kinds is a very low energy frequency. Frequencies attract energies of the same frequencies. If you surround yourself with negativity: anger, frustration, fear, despair, you will attract the same frequencies back. We cannot control the world or each other, but we can control ourselves and, therefore, we have the power to control our energy. Find peace and love instead.

Notice when you are passive aggressive, angry, easily annoyed, or snap at those people around you, negative things will begin to occur around you. This is not a coincidence. You are receiving the same negative energy that you are giving off. Now, notice when you are in a good place in your life, and everything feels positive and peaceful. That is not a coincidence either. Life is but a mirror, reflecting what energy we are exuding from within.

You must try and find a way to tap into that peace and love instead of tapping into the poison. The poison is much easier to tap into; it takes work to tap into peace. It is time to do the work, and you will be so much happier because of it. Try to meet every circumstance with love, compassion, and understanding. You will see the change.

Sending love and light!!

DOES IT SERVE YOU?

Today's lesson of the day is about things that do or do not serve you. If it does not bring you joy, then it does not serve you. If it does not bring you peace, then it does not serve you. If it does not bring beauty into your life, then it does not serve you. If it leaves you helpless, then it does not serve you. If it leaves you powerless, then it does not serve you. If you place someone else above you, taking away your self-worth and power, then it does not serve you. If it brings you anger, then it does not serve you. If it brings you fear, then it does not serve you.

Have in your life what serves you, and get rid of the distractions that stand in your way of happiness. This can be people who try to bring you down, materialistic things that stop you from seeing the beauty in life, technology that distracts – anything that brings you negativity. Because you deserve better.

You have so much power. So much inner strength. You are still standing. You are still here. You have been through so much and yet you wake up every morning to start a new day. You get dressed and you carry on. That is ultimate strength and power. Even though it feels impossible sometimes, the universe will never give you what you cannot handle. And you are proof of that.

So, take a deep breath. Think of something that brings *you* joy. And make sure to do that for yourself at least once a week. Find the time to do whatever that is: eat your favorite food, go to a favorite place in nature, do something creative. Do it for you. Because you have to take care of yourself before you can fully take care of others. Self-care is so important, and so is removing toxicity from your life. You will notice an energy shift, a lightness. Sometimes we forget ourselves. This is your reminder.

Sending love and light!!

APPRECIATION

Today's lesson of the day is to appreciate what you have in your life, not what you do not. You will find there is a lot to be grateful for! Everyone is on a different path. No path is the same as another. What one person is learning may be different than someone else. We are in a world where we feel it is necessary to look at our neighbors, our friends, our family, and compare ourselves to them.

Perhaps one or more of those people live in a bigger house than you, have more expensive cars than you, go on more vacations than you, earn more money at their jobs than you. And what does this do? Creates self-doubt, and the feeling of lack. But something to remember are those who are less fortunate than you.

Others see you and wish they had what you have now. A roof over their head, a car to drive, money to travel, and a decent job to take care of those they love. It is time to look at things differently now because you are much more fortunate than you can even imagine.

Celebrate every win big or small. Sometimes we only notice or look out for the big wins in our lives when there is much to celebrate every day!

Sending love and light!!

SETTING ENERGETIC BOUNDARIES

Today's lesson of the day involves creating and setting boundaries with toxic and negative people in your life. Remember that relationships of all kinds should feel good. They are connections that ultimately should bring you joy. If what you are feeling is the exact opposite of joy when you are around them, it is time to let that person go. The relationship is no longer serving you.

Toxicity is a low energy frequency, and that will only attract more low frequency people and situations into your life. You do not deserve that. It is time to reevaluate your relationships. Do you have those people in your life that make your stomach drop every time you see them? Do they cause a visceral reaction within you?

Your body is trying to give you signals that something is wrong. It is now the moment to listen to what your body is telling you. Are these people superficial and make you feel badly about yourself? Do they treat you like you do not belong? Do they take advantage of you in one or more ways? Listen to your body, and make the decision to put yourself first. Toxicity will only harm you.

Sending love and light!!

THE GROWTH OF A SEED

Today's lesson of the day is that you have planted a seed for your future, and now it is the moment to give it time, and watch it grow. And even though it may grow slowly and you may have a lot to do to reach your goal, every time you get closer remember to be grateful, and celebrate it.

One of the biggest parts of the lesson is to create this opportunity for yourself in service to others without expecting praise instead. We often focus on the accolades and attention we hope to get through a creative idea. How will this get me seen? How much money am I going to make from this idea? Will I finally get respect I deserve from people?

Rather than the praise, the focus needs to be how is it going to help people. How will others benefit from what I have to offer? How can I serve the community with this idea? Keep your original intention for this new idea in your mind. Your intention is the most important part of this new chapter. Remember, you are growing something beautiful. Keep that fire of passion alive inside.

Sending love and light!!

UNLIMITED POTENTIAL

Today's lesson of the day is that you have unlimited potential! Did you know that? You are capable of literally anything! How exciting and amazing is that? If you have an idea of something you want to do, you need to start listening to your intuition. Your intuition is never wrong. When we have amazing ideas and then we start to doubt ourselves, it is our ego getting in the way.

Whenever you have an idea for something or a thought, listen to the little voice that says immediately "Yes, you can!" and "Yes, you will!" and take immediate action! Because not too long after having that amazing idea, your ego will pop in saying "No, you can't!" and "No, you won't!"

Your intuition answers your questions much faster than your ego can. Why? Because our intuition is us listening to our own higher selves and guides. We instinctively know the answers, and it is the first thing we hear. It is when our human minds have time to think about the ideas and thoughts that give us self-doubt.

Follow your gut or your intuition always. It is never wrong. As soon as you have that idea or thought, act on it immediately. Do not allow your ego to ruin something that could be beautiful. We are extremely powerful beings, more powerful than we can even imagine.

So, today, when you think of that amazing idea, listen to that immediate, intuitive response and say "Yes, I can! Yes, I will!" And start making your idea a reality. You are brilliant! You are beautiful! You are powerful! Believe!

Sending love and light!!

THE BALANCE OF CUPS

Today's lesson of the day is a lesson all about balance. Balance in every aspect of our lives. Give and take. If we give too much to our jobs, we cannot possibly give enough to our partners, friends, and loved ones. If we give too much to everyone else, our cups will be nothing but empty with nothing left to give.

So, another question to ask yourself is: what is refilling *your* cup? Giving and receiving go together. Give and take. It is important for both to exist. It creates balance. Make sure to fill someone else's cup, but also make sure that person gives you the refill you need as well.

But a warning: if you are greedy and take too much, remember that your cup can only hold so much. The rest will just spill out over the floor, creating a mess. And that is such a waste when there are other people around you who need their own refill.

We need to open our eyes and give to others in need. This does not mean materialistically. This means giving our time, our compassion, our love, our joy, a listening ear, laughter, and support. And we deserve the same in return. If you achieve this balance, anything and everything is possible. You can reach any goal!

Sending love and light!!

EMOTIONAL BALANCE

Today's lesson of the day is about emotional balance. We are dealing with our emotions constantly from every angle, whether it be relationships, work, or negative forces in our lives. Often, we do not feel like we are on solid ground, as though we are in a storm, on a boat, in the middle of the ocean. This can often give us terrible stress and anxiety.

It is time to take a few big deep breaths. Find a few minutes by yourself to close your eyes. Take a deep breath in for four seconds, hold for four seconds, out for four seconds, and hold for four seconds. Repeat three times. This will recenter yourself. You will find that as you breathe in deeply and release the breath slowly, your anxiety and stress in your stomach will begin to decrease. And the less anxiety and stress in your body, the stronger you will be. How can we make appropriate decisions in our lives when we are emotionally unbalanced?

Once you take a moment for yourself to recenter and breathe, you will find that the answers you seek will be much clearer. With emotional balance, you will find that you have the power to control your own destiny. Anything and everything is possible.

Sending love and light!!

WHAT DO YOU HAVE IN YOUR LIFE?

Today's lesson of the day is about focusing on what you *do* have rather than what you do not have. Sometimes we are so focused on other things we want, we forget to look around us to see all the amazing things we have already.

Take time today (and every day) to reflect on all the positive things you have in your life. Think about your family, your friends, the roof over your head, and food you eat. Think about how you were able to get out of bed this morning despite the challenges in your life, you were given another day on this Earth to learn and grow.

Everything you have in your life is a gift. We need to treat them as gifts because they are precious. If you have forgotten about all the goodness in your life, here is a reminder to stop, close your eyes, and take a mental note of all the amazing gifts you have. Better yet, write down everything you are grateful for and keep it near your bed to read every night before bed and every morning you wake up.

Then, once a week, find a moment to celebrate those wonderful things in your life. Just because. Celebrate in whatever positive way you would like and will bring you and your loved ones joy. Because every day you are given is a gift.

Sending love and light!!

YOUR INCREDIBLE
STRENGTH

Today's lesson of the day is about celebrating your incredible strength! Life here is not easy. It is not exactly meant to be easy for us either. Consider this "Earth school." You are here to learn so your soul can grow, return for harder lessons, and keep learning and growing. But as great as learning and growing sounds, it can be extremely difficult and hard on us. We wonder: Why is this stuff always happening to me? How come my life has always been so hard when everyone else has had it so easy?

It is going to sound difficult to hear, but these things are not happening *to* you, they are happening *for* you. The spirit realm is nothing but positive energy. Negative energy is a man-made creation. We are meant to take the horrible events in our lives and try to turn them into positive lessons to learn and grow from.

This is a very hard pill to swallow because we feel like this is our only life to live, that we literally only have this one chance. But that is far from the truth. You have lived many times before. Ask yourself: How can I learn from this so that I can become stronger? Turn your situation into a positive learning experience, as hard as that can often be when we are grieving loss, in pain, sick, and struggling. This is why we must celebrate our strength. If you have been through a lot, you are more than likely an old soul who has already learned so much that the universe knew you could handle it.

You are strong!! You are a warrior!! Dig deeply inside you for that incredible, ancient, inner strength, because it is there even when you really feel like it is not. And know you are never alone. So many are cheering you on! Celebrate your strength, warrior!! You are more powerful than you could ever imagine!

Sending love and light!!

TEMPTATION AND DESPERATION

Today's lesson of the day is about temptation and relationships. In general, we have a need to make connections. However, sometimes our desire to be with someone is so great, we are willing to ignore red flags. Maybe the person has money, and you are searching for stability. Maybe the person is great with intimacy, and you are in need of affection. Maybe you are hurt from past relationships, and you need someone to help you heal.

Today is about noticing those red flags. Do you want to be with someone because you *need* them, or do you want to be in a relationship because you *want* them to be in your life? Are you interested in them because they fill a void within you? Or are you interested in them because you are already complete, and you want to share your "completeness" with someone?

This is a moment to put the brakes on and think about these questions. Our intuition is never wrong. What is your intuition telling you? We have to look deeply within ourselves; the part of us that lives in the shadows; the part of us we try to ignore. It is an incredibly difficult thing to do, but it is so important to do that so that we can understand ourselves. And once we understand ourselves at a much deeper level, we can begin to understand our choices.

Though it is extremely tempting to rush into something and fill that void, just remember to step back for a moment, take a pause, and ask yourself those important questions. Because if we do not respect ourselves, how can we expect to get respect in return? Love yourself first, because you deserve to! Needing someone takes your power away and gives it to someone else; wanting someone is taking your power back. The rest will fall into place.

Sending love and light!!

RELATIONSHIP PATIENCE

Today's lesson of the day is about patience when looking to get into a relationship. You have so much love to give, and you know that you deserve that same kind of love in return, but it is just not happening yet. You notice others in relationships and keep asking yourself when it will be your turn.

Before we can really dive into a serious relationship, we must do one thing first, and that has to do with loving ourselves. If you have never tried shadow work, the guides highly encourage it. Shadow work is digging deeply into yourself to your shadow parts, the parts of ourselves we hide or try to put on a back shelf so that we never have to look at them. Those are your shadow parts. Your fears and deep traumas that stop you from fully loving yourself.

If you think of yourself as undeserving, you will attract a negative energy in return. And you do not deserve a person who is going to treat you badly or cause you more harm! So, how can we raise our frequencies to a higher energy level? Talking things out with someone is important for your mental health. You may want to talk to a therapist, friends you love and trust, or family members you are highly connected with.

You need to focus on doing the inner work first. Love yourself. Love yourself every day. And once you genuinely feel the warmth of your own love, your energy frequency will raise, and you will be ready to meet someone. Life is not a race. You are exactly where you are meant to be at this very moment. The next step is yours. That means you have the power! Give love to yourself first, and then you can share your love with others! But patience – everything will happen when the time is right.

Sending love and light!!

STEALING FROM ONE TO GIVE TO YOURSELF

Today's lesson of the day is about desperation and stealing from others for your own benefit because you fear you are incapable of it yourself. Now, what in the world does this mean? What are you stealing from others? What are you being deceptive about? Why are you desperate?

First, what are you stealing from others? Is it emotions and love? Is it money? Is it ideas? Is it something creatively? We all fear we are incapable of something, and sometimes we feel that in order to be seen, desperate times call for desperate measures. People are always watching what we do, and that can put an immense amount of pressure and anxiety on ourselves. We panic. We flail around in the water trying to prevent ourselves from drowning.

When we feel incapable in a moment of panic, we may do things we regret later. However, you do not need to steal from someone else to get what you want. You are capable of doing anything that you put your mind to. If you feel you need to be deceitful towards others to get their love and attention, know that you can get their attention just by being you. You have the ability of creating your own ideas!

Being deceitful and stealing from others in various ways is not who you really are. So, it is never too late to make amends with those you have hurt, and turn it into a positive situation. Positive energy will always win. It is like shining a flashlight in a dark room. You got this! Today is a new day with new opportunities. Start fresh and know you can do anything you set your mind to! And do not forget, before we can be honest with others, we must be honest with ourselves.

Sending love and light!!

TAKING THINGS FOR GRANTED

Today's lesson of the day is about taking things for granted. Look around you and notice everything good in your life. When we have an abundance of something, we tend to forget its importance. When you see your family every day, does it become so "usual" that you forget how lucky you are? Have you had money all your life, that you forget how fortunate you are to be in that position? Is your relationship going so well that you stop putting in as much effort?

When, at first, we have something wonderful in our lives, we are grateful for it! But at some point the excitement wears off, and suddenly something we were grateful for becomes regular and usual. Expected. When we are around our family often, live in that nice house for many years, have an abundance of friends – we just expect them to be there.

But as we know in life, nothing is expected, nothing stays the same, and we do not have as much control over things as we hope or think. Never take anything in your life for granted because what is there one day could be gone the next. We need to be grateful for everything that we have in our lives. As much as sometimes we feel like we will be in this life forever, we will not. What begins must end.

So, when you see your family, you see all the time, get that excitement back. Bring back the gratitude. Because it will not always be like this. Change is always inevitable. When you see your family, be present in that moment and grateful to have that moment. When you walk into your house, look around you, and be grateful you have shelter. When you see your friends, be grateful you have people in your life who care about you, and vice versa. Never take anything for granted. Always gratitude.

Sending love and light!!!

NURTURING LOVE

Today's lesson of the day is about nurturing the love you have for others and taking action by showing that love for them. This is about family, friend, and romantic relationships specifically. We all have that magical way of making others feel important, loved, and wanted. Now it is time to put that magic to action. After all, our soul's purpose in this "Earth school" is to better love ourselves and love others and spread that love around to as many people as we can.

So, what have you done to show love to your loved ones lately? When you close your eyes, think of that question, and really concentrate on it, your intuition will give you the answer. If you have not shown others love lately, perhaps you are stressed or anxious about other things, perhaps you are working a lot. If that is the case, those moments you are with loved ones are even more precious. How can we start to show our love to our loved ones today?

Maybe you show love in giving your time to them. Maybe you all cook a big dinner together. Maybe you have a movie night with buckets of popcorn. Maybe it is going on an outing somewhere. Maybe it is a long hug. Maybe it is starting a new tradition. Maybe it is continuing old traditions. Maybe it is having a dance party to let off steam. Maybe it is having a sleepover in the family room where you can break all the rules regardless of your age. Maybe it is giving someone flowers or their favorite chocolates. Maybe it is simply telling someone you love them.

Show the love today. It is never too late, and there is never a wrong time. With spreading love, you are spreading joy and joy is infectious. And we all need more of that in our lives.

Sending love and light!!

REAL MAGIC

Today's lesson of the day is about noticing and looking at the magic around you. The guides are not talking about magic shown in movies or in books, but the magic of the universe that is all around us constantly. Magic comes in many forms. Have you ever prayed or made a wish, and it came true? Have you ever made a wish, but it did not happen until everything was aligned perfectly first and suddenly you had an "Oh, I see now!" moment?

There are no coincidences in this world. Everything happens when it is supposed to happen. As though something is always there guiding us so we stay on our right path. And we do! That is magic. The beautiful things around you are pure magic. Your family, your friendships, your relationships? Were you not searching for someone in your life and suddenly "poof!" there they are, and you ask yourself "where did they come from?" That is magic.

Look at your beautiful pets in your homes. They are your guardians who were given to you for specific purposes. Some pets are given to us for protection, others companionship, comic relief, affection, and most importantly love. That is magic. So, treat your protective guardians like the royalty that they are because as much as you think you found them, they were the ones waiting for you when the time was right. The universe always has a beautiful and positive plan for us. Even when things are not going well, sometimes we must knock down an old building so we can rebuild it up again stronger, bigger, and on a much better foundation. That is magic.

Magic is always around us and always for our good. Close your eyes and feel it surrounding you. That tingling, warm, positive feeling is the magic flowing through you. It is also a beautiful day to make a wish, so make a wish, you beautiful soul! Know you are always heard!

Sending love and light!!

BE THE CHILD

Today's lesson of the day is if you have a new fun idea of creating something, doing something exciting, or starting a new fun project, today is the day to begin it! It is time to bring the child-self out to come out and play! You have everything inside you needed to begin, and today is the perfect day to do just that! Sometimes we let work or outside sources beyond our control get in our way.

Today it is the moment to say, "it is time." Do it for you! Have fun with it and enjoy the ride! It is time to bring back the child in us because it is okay to be a child again. In fact, you should be. Just because we are older does not mean you cannot recreate that magic again!

Whatever it is, today is the day to start putting fun ideas and projects in your head into reality! Who says you cannot be a kid again? Age is only a number. How do you feel inside? So, bring out that inner child today! You will be thankful and happy you did!

Sending love and light!!!

PROVIDING FOR YOUR FAMILY

Today's lesson of the day is about providing for your family. Raising a family is not easy. There are constant challenges that arise on a daily basis, sometimes even on an hourly or minute basis. But even when things are at its craziest, you are still strong enough to manage it because you already have, and you will again in the future.

You are the person or couple who not only have a family to raise, but you are trying to balance your life as an individual as well. Your work life, your married or partnered life, and your mental health, all while trying to be good role models for your children. Know you are doing the best you can, and your best must be good enough. Do not look to how others live. Regardless of your circumstances, you are doing it, and you are doing the best you can!

Give yourself some grace because no one is perfect, and we all make mistakes now and will continue to do so. So, take the burden of perfection off your shoulders because it is unattainable. You are doing the absolute best you can, and that makes you a rockstar! You not only provide for your kids and pets, but you also surround them with as much love as possible. Remember, love makes you wealthy!

Your children will always remember the love they were given over anything else. So, take a moment or a few moments today to step back and be proud of the job you are doing! It is not easy, but you are doing it with love, and that is all that matters!

Sending love and light!!

TEAMWORK

Today's lesson of the day is about teamwork to reach your goals. We cannot always do it alone. Sometimes we need help and support from others so we can reach our destination. Asking for help or knowing it is time to collaborate with others is not being weak; asking for help to get the job done is showing your strength.

If you have an idea about something but are unsure about how to do it and you need assistance, now is the day to do it! Collaborate on something! Sometimes it takes two, or three, or a village! Strength is asking for help when you need it.

Maybe this has to do with a home project or something to do with work or maybe it is something creative you have in mind or perhaps it is asking someone to be a workout partner to keep each other motivated. Whatever is in your mind, it is time to work together! Today is the day!

Sending love and light!!

YOUR LIFE PATH

Today's lesson of the day is to understand life paths. What does this mean? Aren't we already on a life path? Isn't that just life in general? In a way, but it is more than that. A life path is your spiritual pathway. The reason you came here to "Earth school." We are here to learn many lessons so that our soul energies can grow. We grow and learn much quicker coming back here time after time.

So, where does your life path come into play? It is your overall mission during school. Besides learning and teaching lessons, ask the questions: what are you doing to help and heal others and spread love? What are you doing to share your gifts with the world? How are you serving others? What are you doing to contribute to raising the world's energy frequency?

Our purpose here is to learn and teach lessons to each other, spread love, help and heal others in the process, and use our gifts to the fullest. This includes sharing your experiences with others so they can learn from you. Do something kind and selfless for others. Spread some joy to someone who needs it. It is amazing what a kind word or gesture can do for another person. You may inspire them to do the same for someone else and so on. Love is beautiful, and love is healing. It is amazing how an act of love can spread so quickly. You create positive waves that just keep creating more waves and more waves.

So, what is your life path? How can you start making those positive waves today? What are you going to do to keep spreading love to those around you or even those you do not know? It is also another day to make a wish! So please do!! They are always listening!

Sending love and light!!

FORGING AHEAD

Today's lesson of the day is when life gets hard, and you feel like you are constantly being tested, you have the strength within you to forge ahead! There are times when it feels like we have so many things being thrown at us. When it rains, it often pours. This can be extremely tough because it feels like we cannot breathe.

This is where grounding yourself is extremely important. Close your eyes, take a deep breath in for four seconds, hold for four seconds, breathe out for four seconds, and hold for four seconds. Repeat three times. Imagine roots from your feet growing into the Earth. Imagine positive energy and light entering through the roots and filling your body. Then, after some time, open your eyes and forge ahead. Know that these moments will come and go quickly. So, give yourself that boost to push through to the finish line, because you *do* have it in you. You are much stronger than you think!

If you feel like you are constantly being tested, remember that you really are. We will always have things being thrown at us because that is how we learn and grow the most. Sometimes the tests are hard. But no test is impossible. You already have the knowledge inside you to get yourself through it. And like all tests, they only last a short period of time.

After your "test" is over, it is time to practice self-care. Remember to be kind to yourself. Do something that brings you joy. When your cup is drained, it is important to refill it. You *will* get through the hard times. You know you will because you have before, and you will again! Stay strong, warrior! You are never alone!

Sending love and light!!

ACCOMPLISHMENT

Today's lesson of the day is about your incredible superpower to accomplish anything you put your mind to. If you have the want to change something in your life that will make you happy, just know that you are more than capable of doing it! The power lives inside of each of us. All you need to do is sit with yourself for a moment, meditate, even journal about it if you wish, and ask yourself the important question: "what do I need to do to feel happy and fulfilled?" And your intuition will give you the answer.

Trust that your intuition is correct because our intuition is correct a hundred percent of the time. Your intuition is your magical superpower that everyone has access to at any moment if you are open to hearing what it has to say.

What will make you happy and fulfilled in your life? What will bring you joy? Whatever that is, you have the power within you to make it happen! Our ego makes us believe otherwise, and this is a reminder to shove that ego to the side. The ego will only create self-doubt and fear within us. Who needs more of that in our lives?

So, take that step towards happiness today! Choose positivity over negativity. Optimism over pessimism. Joy over sadness. Love over hate. Look in the mirror and see your beauty inside and out. You are capable of anything and everything! So, get out there and make it happen!

Sending love and light!!

HEARTBREAK

Today's lesson of the day is about heartbreak with a loved one. This message is mostly geared towards romantic partnerships: unexpected breakups, relationships ending in divorce, or our partners who unexpectedly or expectedly transition over. We meet people who we connect with on a deeper level, and we think it is forever. We begin to think of all possibilities and the want or need for companionship. You build something with the other person, and then something happens that drastically changes the trajectory of your life.

You are thrown into a life change that you never wanted or imagined for yourself. The relationship you once had has now almost ceased to exist. Now that partnership is just a memory, and you begin to not only grieve the ending of the relationship, but you begin to grieve the life you thought you were supposed to have.

But know that even through your pain and suffering whether a relationship ended or it is a relationship lost, you are never dead inside. Think of a major surgery. You have this surgery, and surgeries of all types are not fun. There is a time of healing from it. And during that time the pain can be excruciating. But remember that all pain is temporary, though memories remain.

The pain will become less and less, but the memories will always be there. How do we change the negative into a positive? We ask ourselves the important question: what did we learn, and how can we grow from it in a positive way? You have learned more than you know. Remember that we are individuals first and foremost. That individual is still inside of you. It is time to reintroduce yourself to yourself, and love that person again. The future is full of never-ending possibilities. Give yourself the opportunity to see what those possibilities are.

Sending love and light!!

CELEBRATE YOUR DREAMS

Today's lesson of the day is about celebrating your dreams. What does this mean? Why celebrate something that has not happened yet? Dreams come from deep within. Your soul's urge. It is what lights your pilot light and keeps you going. If you could look through a window of your soul, what is the one thing that would make your soul happy? What pulls you? Is it being creative in some way? Is it helping others? What are your future dreams and desires? What would make you feel complete and fulfilled?

Once you know the answer to that question, it is time to celebrate it. But why celebrate your dreams? Because they are gifts that are given to you. Dreams tell us that anything and everything is possible. They show us that we can reach any goal if we work towards it and stay focused. That obstacles in your way are just challenges and nothing more.

Celebrate all the possibilities. Because dreams are never unreachable. Dreams are the beginnings of manifestation. It is within you! And do not forget it is about the journey, not the finish line. Enjoy the process of getting there because you will enjoy and appreciate the finish line much more when you get there. So, celebrate your dreams, because in turn you are really celebrating yourself as well!

Sending love and light!!

PAYING IT FORWARD

Today's lesson of the day is about paying it forward. Helping others you do not even know to make them feel a sense of joy and happiness they may not have felt before. What a beautiful way to help raise the positive energy frequency of the collective!! Did you know that helping someone by brightening their day creates a ripple effect? If you throw a stone in the water, notice how the water ripples outwards from every direction. Now imagine the rock is your love and kindness. It is the same effect.

Once that person feels the amazing frequency of your love, which is the highest energy frequency there is, the ripples will continue because they will, in turn, do something of love and kindness for someone else. The ripples of love will reach more people than you could ever imagine!

Just one act of kindness and love for someone today can be that powerful! How incredible is it that we have that kind of ability? Because we are all divine beings who have that magic within us. We are capable of anything! Remember, though, paying it forward is a completely selfless act of love and kindness. An act where you do not expect anything in return. You are not getting anything out of it other than the joy of being able to do something beautiful for someone else. Some even do their acts of kindness anonymously. That is up to you.

Today is the day! What selfless act of kindness will you do for someone else? How will you spread joy and love to an unsuspecting person? You will walk away with joy and love yourself just knowing you have started a ripple that will continue onto many others!

Sending love and light!!

ABUSIVE RELATIONSHIPS

Today's lesson of the day is about abusive relationships. If you have ever asked yourself: Why am I being treated this way? Why is this person so horrible to me? Before we can address the other person, we need to address ourselves first. This is where energy frequencies come into play. Like attracts like; frequencies attract frequencies. The question you need to ask yourself is what state of mind were you in at the time of meeting this person?

Is this victim blaming? Absolutely not. It is important to get to the root cause. Because it is all related. At the time of the meeting were you depressed? Had you been rejected multiple times before? Were you in need of companionship? Were you afraid of loneliness? Do you feel you deserve it? Frequencies matter. If we are at a very low energy frequency ourselves, we will attract an equally low energy frequencied person in return.

But you deserve better! You deserve all the love in the world! But before you can find love outside of yourself, you need to love yourself first. Imagine: love is a massive ball of positive, beautiful light energy inside. Imagine it filling every inch of you inside and out. This beautiful light then shoots out of you in all directions, touching other lives around you. All that love will attract the same energy to you. If you are in an abusive relationship, those people are keeping you at their low vibration, so they have power over you. But *you* have the power. You have always had the power inside you! Take your power back from your abuser and get out of there regardless of how difficult it will be.

Find a plan. Find support from others who can lift you up. You are not alone. Strength is asking for help when you need it. It is time to see those chains disappear. The beautiful seed has now been planted. It is time to act.

Sending love and light!!

INVESTING FOR YOUR FUTURE

Today's lesson of the day is about investing money in some way for your future. Sometimes we only think about the *now* part of life, and not necessarily when we are older. Not everyone has a pension or TRS, not everyone has a 401K, not everyone has invested in their futures. What will happen to us after we retire? Or can we ever retire? Start considering investing in your future if you have not already.

For example, open a Roth IRA account with a company where you can watch your interest grow much faster than a savings account. There is no set amount to start your investment, and the investment experts at these companies can help you decide where to invest your money safely and securely.

Only put in an amount each month that you can add easily without causing any monetary harm to yourself or your family, and know that you can always change the amount you put in at any time. Always invest responsibly.

Why are the guides talking about money today when money literally means nothing to them on the other side? Because our spirit guides look out for us! They are literally here to guide us so that we can have a better life here. Unfortunately, on this planet, we need money to survive. So, this is a way of helping ourselves prepare for our futures, and there is never a bad time to start! Talk to a friend who knows a lot about investing or contact an investment company where they can assist you!

Sending love and light!!

TAKE ON CHALLENGES

Today's lesson of the day is about taking on challenges head on! We are faced with challenges every single day. Some are small challenges like changing a light bulb or large challenges like taking on a completely new job at work or moving to another place, etc. Either way, today is the day to face those challenges with positivity and acceptance.

Why acceptance? Because throughout our lives we are given these tests, especially the big challenges, that will strengthen our soul energies. Since the only reason we are here on this planet is to learn, grow, and love, it makes perfect sense that we should accept these challenges in our lives and forge ahead! Remember, as hard as it is to say it, our souls grow the most through the hard challenges.

Challenges are opportunities to help us in the end. They often take hard work and take time. Just know you have the upper hand. These major life challenges always occur when there is a major life fork in the road. It is a time of big decision for you!

Just remember that you got this! You have the courage and strength to get through anything when you take a moment to breathe and put your mind to it! And like all challenges, they are not forever. So, go and get it, warrior!!

Sending love and light!!

CLUES FOR CHANGE

Today's lesson of the day is when your spirit guides give you clues to change your path, listen. We all have dreams and expectations in our lives. Our dreams and desires begin at a very young age. We see ourselves being successful at something very specific. We might see ourselves in a fairytale relationship. We might see ourselves in our dream job. We might see ourselves living in a specific place either another state or even another country.

You follow your heart completely. You do the necessary things to get your goals. You get your partner. You get your dream job. You move to that amazing place that was going to make you happy. But then something starts to shift. Years later things start going wrong. Your beautiful relationship is now toxic. Your dream job is making you unhappy. The place that you moved to for new possibilities is leaving you empty with less and less hope every day.

Why is this happening? We are all on a specific path that we agreed to before coming here. It does not mean we do not have free will to do what we want, but we are all meant to be on a certain path. Sometimes we get so stubborn or blinded by possibility that we ignore the signs from our guides to take a pause and reevaluate. Our guides will first start to give us nice, subtle hints trying to help us get back on track, but we ignore them. Then they start to give us even more obstacles in our lives.

At this point, you may think your guides are punishing you. But that is not the case. Remember, your guides want the best for you. They are simply trying to get you back on track, and this is your time to start listening. This is your moment to take a breath, take a pause, and take the hint. You have an amazing path you are meant to be on, and they will slowly guide you back to it. Trust.

Sending love and light!

WALKING AWAY

Today's lesson of the day is that if something is not serving you, you need to walk away. This could be friendships, relationships, jobs, and even toxic family environments. Sometimes we get so stuck in life because we feel we must be in these negative situations. "That is life, I guess. I am just meant to be a doormat for other people to walk all over." If people are taking advantage of you, remember that that is not okay. No one should ever be taking advantage of another person.

Perhaps your friendship or relationship is very one sided; they only contact you when they need you for something. After they get what they want from you, you do not hear from them again until the next time. When you are at work, and you feel unappreciated. You do not feel seen or heard. You are constantly going above and beyond, and no one notices or thanks you for all the work you are doing.

Then it is time to walk away. Find people who *do* appreciate you. Give and take. You do not need people or jobs in your life who drain you and give nothing in return. You are more than just a number to a large corporation. You are a beautiful, bright light. And people are lucky to know you!

Have that strength and courage to walk away when you have to. Know your worth. As you fill other people's cups selflessly, make sure your cup is being filled too. And that is not being selfish. Remember, we are of no good to anyone if we are completely drained of all the energy we have!

Sending love and light!!

HEALING PAST WOUNDS

Today's lesson of the day is about healing wounds from the past for a much more hopeful future. There are times when we have been hurt so badly in the past that we are stuck. We are unable to move forward in the present. Was it a past trauma? Was it a past mistake you made that hurt others? What was it that has stopped you from moving forward?

This is the day to start that healing process. If this is something that goes really deep, consider help from a professional who can guide you on your healing journey. Remember, we are not our traumas or our past mistakes. We cannot be defined by these things. If you have made a mistake that may have hurt other people in the past, know that it is time to let that go. We are not defined by our mistakes. We are defined by the love we have given to others. We are always defined by the positive not the negative in our lives.

Keeping these feelings inside will only bottle it up, and it will come out in unhealthy ways such as addictions to dissociate or emotional explosions towards others. It is time to face the darker parts of ourselves we are ashamed of or fear so that we can move into a healthier and happier and more positive tomorrow.

Nothing is impossible! Know that you have the power and strength within you to begin the healing process! You deserve the best future! So do not give up hope! Let us start that healing process today! It is also a perfect day to make a wish! Make one now!!

Sending love and light!!

MENTAL HEALTH FOCUS

Today's lesson of the day is that we need to start focusing or continuing to focus on our mental health. Sometimes we feel like we are prisoners in our own brains. And that can turn life into a massive struggle. Depression, anxiety, and stress (among others) can hold us hostage where it cripples us on a daily basis. You may not even want to get out of bed today, and you do not feel like you are in control of your own body.

The first thing you need to do is give yourself some grace. Depression, stress, and anxiety can do a number on us, not only mentally but physically as well. You may find you are unable to sleep. You might have horrible aches and pains in the body. You may find you get sick more often.

If this is a usual occurrence for you, and you are struggling often, it is time to seek help. You do not have to go through this alone. Courage and strength is getting the help you need. And you deserve to live a better life. So, if you need extra support, there are many options for you, and you can choose what is best for you!

If your depression, anxiety, and stress is a short-term issue, take a moment to pause, breathe some deep breaths, find something beautiful and positive to focus on in that moment, and know that nothing lasts forever. Perhaps working out is a stress reliever for you. Maybe it is baking something fun. Maybe you need a night out with a friend to unwind. Maybe you need a professional massage. Whatever will help you, you got this! We all go through moments where we feel out of control of our own selves, but we can take our control back! You got this, warrior!

Sending love and light!!

REUNITING

Today's lesson of the day is about reuniting with close friends and family you may not have seen for a while due to a disagreement or upset. Is there a family member or close friend you have not spoken to lately because something they did angered or frustrated you? Perhaps something was said and you could not get over it, but rather than talking things out, you have allowed things to fester over time?

This is not about who is right and who is wrong. This is about having the courage to speak up when you are hurt or upset. A lot of times you will find that what was said was not said in malice at all, and perhaps there was a misunderstanding. If you do not talk things out and say how you feel, it will only bottle up inside you and combust later. You may feel like you are "getting back" at the person by ignoring them and giving the silent treatment, but who you are really hurting is yourself.

When you keep anger and frustration inside of you and you do not resolve the issue, it causes more stress and anxiety and anger in your body. These lower energy frequencies will wreak havoc on you. Not only will you bring negative energy in your life where things will go wrong, it will also cause damage to your body. Stress, anxiety, and anger can cause headaches, stomach aches, sleeplessness, illnesses, etc. It is much better to release these negative energies.

This is the time to resolve these conflicts. Have a conversation with the person you are upset with. Have a calm dialogue. If the person refuses to see how they hurt you, is that someone you want in your life? Often, when you talk things out, the person will see they have caused some harm to you and apologize. Do not allow negative emotions to fester; it will only cause you more harm. Talk things out and move forward, and you will be on a much healthier path!

Sending love and light!!

TAKING ADVANTAGE OF THE LESS FORTUNATE

The lesson of the day is about wealthy people taking advantage of those less fortunate. No matter how much wealth you have accumulated over the years, it does not make you better than anyone else. This does not give someone the right to do whatever they want to another individual. If you happen to be one of the few who happen to be well off financially, it is time to look at people as people again. You have knowingly affected their well-being. What does not matter much to you could mean the world to someone else.

Did you destroy a company to get even or have financial gain? Did you create a toxic environment on purpose to hurt certain individuals? Did you come through like a tornado and leave everything in ruins behind you?

Sometimes when we have that much money, we forget that people are important. Selfishness may get you places on this planet, but it will not do you any good when you get back "home" at the end of your human life. Your life will be measured in the love you have given, and your wealth will mean nothing.

Now is the time for change. It is time to make amends to those lives you have hurt in some way. Instead of wreaking havoc on others, create positive environments. Use your wealth to help raise the world's energy frequency and not just for personal gain. Think about others and give back. Remember who you were before you changed into the person you are today and bring that person back. It is never too late to make a change for the better, and there is no better time to start than today! It is time to ground yourself again. Once you do, you will do a world of good.

Sending love and light!!

GROWING YOUR INTUITIVE GIFTS

Today's lesson of the day is about growing your intuitive gifts! This is a very magical lesson because intuitive magic is real. And the best part about intuition is we all have it in different ways. Some get feelings and premonitions, some can read energies of others, some are clairvoyant, some are mediums who can connect with those who have passed.

We were all born with some kind of incredible intuitive gift, but we were often taught at an early age that those things do not exist and that talking about intuitive gifts were the work of the Devil. People from the beginning of time have been hung or burned at the stake just for having these natural gifts. But times have changed. People are exploring. And the higher your energy frequencies, the stronger your abilities grow.

Children from ages zero to five years old have these abilities very strongly. Listen to your children, and tell them that it is normal, and not to be afraid of it. If they tell you a woman was in their room, then there was a woman in their room. People who have passed can sense when someone has these abilities because it is all energy. These are gifts to be harnessed, not to be ignored.

It is time to believe in magic, because magic is real. We cannot always explain everything, and that is okay. Study it, learn about it, develop your God given abilities! Start with regular meditation. Raise your energy frequencies so you can have an all-access pass to your natural gift! It is now time to explore your intuition! Your life will change for the better! Stay completely open, and allow yourself to reconnect to Source (God) in the best way!

Sending love and light!!

STARTING NEW TRADITIONS

Today's lesson of the day is about starting new traditions that bring you joy. Remember back when you were a child, and there were traditions that were passed down from generation to generation? For many of us, that has brought us a sense of nostalgia as we have gotten older. And sometimes we even take those old traditions and pass them down ourselves.

But every new tradition has to start somewhere! And perhaps that new tradition starts with you! What kind of new tradition would you like to start this year? Does it have to do with a certain holiday? Does it revolve around someone's birthday? Is it making pancakes on a Saturday? Is it making homemade hot chocolate every time it snows? Is it going to a craft fair every season with friends or family?

Your new tradition can be anything that warms your heart and brings you and others joy! The new tradition that you and others will remember forever and may even be passed down to other generations! There are no right or wrong answers! What new tradition can you start this year to add to the magic of life? Something you cannot wait to do every week, every month, or every year. Maybe you want to create multiple new traditions! Anything and everything is possible!

Traditions are something you can create yourself or with others! Once you create them, make a point to keep them alive. And after many, many years that pass by, you will look fondly on the day you started your new tradition(s), and smile.

Sending love and light!!

CREATING YOUR DESTINY

Today's lesson of the day is if you live your life in truth and balance, you can create your own destiny. Let us break this down so that we can understand this further. What is truth? Truth is living your authentic self. It is not pretending to be something or someone else. It makes us vulnerable and honest not only with others, but also ourselves. But know there is no one like you in the entire universe. We all bring a special and unique ray of light, and each of us make a bigger difference than you could ever imagine! Keep discovering who you truly are. That is part of our mission. You are nothing but love and light!

Balance is equally as important! If we are unbalanced, we can feel uneasy, anxious, stressed, frustrated, helpless; like we are about to drown. These negative energy frequencies can wreak havoc on us. But there is a way that we can keep our heads above water.

Look at all the aspects of your life: work, parenting, family, chores and errands, and self-care. What parts of these are you ignoring, and which ones are you giving all of yourself to? The answer is often that we forget about ourselves. Self-care. How can we change that? What can we do for ourselves daily and weekly that will refill our cup? Once you practice self-care, you will feel so much more balanced in life.

When you achieve truth and balance, you will find that anything and everything is possible! Take one step at a time, and you will reach any goal you have set for yourself! You are beautiful, you are magical, you are unstoppable.

Sending love and light!!

RELATIONSHIP
BREAKDOWN

Today's lesson of the day is about breaking down relationship walls that were not built on solid ground, and knowing when to start from scratch or walk away. Relationships are a big part of everyone's lives. But not all relationships are as strong as people would hope for. Perhaps your family life growing up was not very loving or supportive. Perhaps your friendship with someone is one sided. Perhaps your romantic relationship was built on looks. Or perhaps your relationship is lacking in many different areas all together.

Sometimes it is time to reevaluate and see what is really going on that is making you unhappy with the relationship. How is this relationship serving you? Does it bring you joy? Does it bring you peace? Happiness? If not, it may be time to make a decision.

If your relationship was not built on solid ground to begin with, the longer we work hard at building the wobbly structure higher, the more of a possibility of the structure collapsing to the ground. It is time to tear those walls down and decide if you want to rebuild or walk away from the relationship. But if you rebuild, make sure to create that solid foundation first, and that takes time. But everything is possible if the people involved want it to be. It is about working together as a team!

Sending love and light!!

TRY SOMETHING NEW

Today's lesson of the day is to get out there and do something fun you have never done before! Have you ever made a list in your mind of fun things you have always wanted to do? Well, today is the day to do it! It is a brand-new day where anything is possible, so what are you going to do with this new day of opportunity?

Maybe there is a new restaurant you have always wanted to try! Maybe you have wanted to go horseback riding all your life! Maybe you have been wanting to redecorate your house! Maybe there is a movie you have wanted to see! Maybe you have always wanted to go to a comedy club!

Whatever it is, today is the day to do something fun that you have never had the opportunity to do before! Sometimes we are so busy adulting that we forget that we have the child within us that wants to get out and play!

Age is just a number! Bringing out the child from within will help you to rediscover yourself. Life does not have to be so serious all the time!

So, today, get out there. Be silly! Let the child from inside come out, and have the fun you deserve to have! What fun new experience are you going to have today?

Sending love and light!!

A LEVEL HEAD AND
DECISION MAKING

Today's lesson of the day is about staying calm and levelheaded so that you can make important decisions. This is easier said than done because when it comes to having to make life changing decisions, and perhaps having to make them quickly, we can often get into a panic mode that forces us to think with our ego rather than our intuitions.

This life changing decision could be if you need to move somewhere quickly due to a certain reason, or whether to take a job or not after losing another one, or if someone is in a negative or abusive relationship, or if someone is in any other negative situation they need to get out of fast. We immediately go into fight or flight mode making all decisions we make based on us panicking and our anxicty.

Firstly, remove yourself from the situation for a moment. Close your eyes and take some deep breaths to reground yourself. No decisions can be good decisions when you are surrounded by negative energy that causes you to panic. Once you feel calm and no longer as anxious, ask yourself the important question: how can I best resolve the issue? Your intuition will give you the answer rather than our egos drowning the answer out, causing more stress.

Remember that all big decisions can change our lives, so it is good to come up with a calm and rational plan so that you can manage everything in your mind. Nothing is impossible. Always ground yourself by breathing deeply and calming your mind and body. Once you are calm, you will be able to make an appropriate decision that will be best for you. Trust in your intuitive judgment. Your intuition is always right and is always there for you! You got this!!

Sending love and light!!

ROMANTIC EFFORT

Today's lesson of the day is about making sure you are putting in enough effort into your romantic relationships. Sometimes we can say our romantic partners are not giving their all into the relationship. It feels very one sided, and you are doing most of the work for two people. But what happens when it is us that need to put in more effort?

In those moments, we need to call ourselves out and put ourselves in check. Deep down we know if we are doing the bare minimum or not. But it takes two people to make a relationship work. It must be equal. Give and take. Without us giving enough of ourselves to the other, the workload will not be evenly distributed, and the relationship will be unbalanced. If we give too much, we are doing all the work, and it is again, unbalanced.

Are you focusing too much on other things in your life rather than this partnership? How can you create more of a balance in your life so you can dedicate more time to keeping the fire alive with your partner? And if it is not outside forces creating a barrier between the two of you, what is stopping you from giving your all into the relationship? Are you not as interested as you thought? Are you dealing with past traumas? Is it all of the above?

Communication is the key. If you are invested in this relationship, it is time to have some conversations and be open and honest with each other. Perhaps the unbalance is short lived. Talk to each other so everyone is on the same page, and that way you will still be a team. Because without teamwork, the relationship simply cannot exist. It takes two!

Sending love and light!!

HEALTH CHECKUPS

Today's lesson of the day is all about going to the doctor once a year to get your health checked out. We only have one body this lifetime, so we must make sure we are doing what we can to protect it. They say that our body is a temple, and they are not wrong. But sometimes fear can get in the way of our choices to go to the doctor for our regular checkups and physicals.

How long has it been since your last physical examination? Two years? Three years? Much longer than that? It is time to gather up strength and make that appointment. It is so important to know what is going on with our bodies so we can stay around for as long as possible to continue to learn and grow and love.

Fear of the doctor is a real thing. White coat syndrome. Blood pressures rise, anxiety, stress. But sometimes we have to do the uncomfortable things so that we can be happy and healthy in the end. There is also fear of outcomes such as a diagnosis from a test result; some would rather not know about something than find out something is wrong. But we must have that incredible strength we all have deep inside. Knowing results can save your life.

So, keep up to date with your checkups. Have your yearly physical. Schedule it today if you have not. We want you to stay around for as long as possible, so start making your health a priority today!

Sending love and light!!

RELATIONSHIP ENDINGS AND BEGINNINGS

Today's lesson of the day is when one relationship ends, it allows for a new beginning of another. When we are in a relationship with someone, we think and hope that it will work out. In the end we are all looking for companionship in some form. It is a natural desire. But when that relationship ends in whatever way it ends, we feel disoriented and lost. Often, we feel hopeless, helpless, and depressed.

But remember that every wound heals over time, and nothing is forever. Pain is not forever. Something must die so that something new can be reborn. It is the cycle of life and can be applied to every aspect of our lives. When one chapter ends, a new chapter begins. And this new chapter has limitless possibilities for you.

Perhaps the relationship you thought was forever, was only meant to teach you lessons for a short time. Perhaps you are supposed to meet someone in this new chapter. Maybe it will be an even stronger emotional connection than you ever had before.

We never fully understand why things happen to us throughout our lives, but know that there are no coincidences. Everything happens for a reason. It is our job to decipher what those reasons are so we can learn and grow. Perhaps in the last chapter you were the caterpillar, and in this new chapter you become the butterfly.

Sending love and light!!

BETRAYAL OF A LOVED ONE

Today's lesson of the day is about betraying someone you love. We are all human, and we all make mistakes throughout our lives. Perhaps you have done something that you regret. Maybe you lied to someone you love about something or you did something that you are hiding from them.

Remember that we are not our mistakes. We are not measured in the negative things we do; we are measured in the love that we give. We also cannot control how other people react to what we have done. Will we lose a relationship or a friendship? Possibly. But keeping these heavy, negative things inside of us is the real problem because it will eat us alive.

Today is the day to come clean and tell the person we have hidden things from the truth. The truth will finally remove that burden from your shoulders. Will it cause some pain and hurt? Possibly, yes. These things are never easy. However, once a wound is open, you can finally allow it to heal. If you have lost a relationship or friendship in the process, then you have learned a very difficult and valuable lesson for the future.

Some lessons are extremely difficult to learn, but all lessons learned are positive ones. Learning is a very positive energy. Once we learn the lessons, they help us grow. And growing is a part of life here. You are stronger than you think! Sometimes Earth school is a big challenge. This is just one of those times.

Sending love and light!!

A NEW GREAT IDEA

Today's lesson of the day is bringing a new great idea to life!! You have been thinking about doing something for quite some time. A new idea! A new concept! It has been on your mind for a while now and you just have not started it yet.

Perhaps it is a new idea of starting your own business! Perhaps it is writing that story that has been in your mind for so long! Perhaps it is a way to make your life or someone else's life better or easier! Whatever this idea is, it is a good one, and one to celebrate!!

We fear the unknown. We fear what we do not already see in front of us. We are afraid of putting in effort and not getting anything in return. Our ego creeps in: what if I am wasting my time? What if this does not work? Is this a stupid idea? What if no one likes it? Will I make any money from it?

It is time to throw your ego aside today! To throw that caution to the wind, because you have a great idea and you are onto something! So, take that beautiful idea that has been in your mind and turn it into reality! This is your sign that today is the day! We are all divine beings, and with divination comes magic. We have that in us!! If you have that new idea, it is time to make it a reality!! No fear. Just joy! And celebrate it because it deserves to be celebrated!! 11:11. Divine guidance.

Sending love and light!!

TAKING ACTION

Today's lesson of the day is about your dreams, and to start taking action! What have you always wanted? Is it a certain career? Is it owning a home? Is it something creative you have always wanted to do? Is it traveling to a certain place you have always wanted to go? Is it wanting a pet to be a part of your family?

Write down your dream list. Everything and anything that you have always wanted in your life. It is time to tackle one of your dreams one at a time. As humans, we want everything right now and we want everything fast. But life is not a fast-food restaurant. These things take time to manifest. Some dreams are more long term and take longer to manifest, but that does not mean it will not happen. When you plant a tree, it takes time for it to grow, but it will in time!

Today is the day to begin to manifest one of your dreams on your list. How do you do that? Magic is all around us. You simply need to start doing it, and make it happen. If you want a dream career, start researching what you need to do to get it! If you need to take a class or two, start signing up! If you want to travel to that dream place, start saving money every paycheck to make that happen!

Our spirit guides are always working hard for us, and they are rooting for us to succeed. But we have to meet them halfway. They are not just going to put what we want in front of us and say, "Here you are!" So, dive into the work today. You are more than capable of getting everything you dream of!! It is time to manifest some amazing things, because *you* are amazing!!!

Sending love and light!!

COUNT YOUR BLESSINGS

Today's lesson of the day is about taking something you have for granted. Sometimes we forget how lucky we are. We are blessed with so many amazing and wonderful things in our lives that sometimes we just expect them to be there. But what about the people outside looking in? There are so many people around you who wish they had what you have.

Maybe you have the family someone else does not. Maybe you have the career someone else wishes they had. Maybe you have been fortunate enough to see the world when someone else has not. Maybe you have been healthy with no medical problems all your life when someone else has not. Maybe you are skating through life while someone else is struggling every single day. Maybe you were able to get out of bed today when someone else could not.

We tend to go through life and have our own experiences, but we often do not stop and pause a moment to be grateful for everything we have or have done in our lives. Not everyone has been given the life or opportunities that you have, and that makes you very fortunate. So, let us take a moment to be grateful.

We are all more fortunate than others when it comes to something. What are you grateful for? Make a list of everything you are grateful for, and read that list every single day. Sometimes our lives are so crazy we forget. It is time to remember. You will have more on your list than you ever thought you would!

Sending love and light!!

ACCEPTING HELP WHEN NEEDED

Today's lesson of the day is not to be too proud to accept help when you really need it. A lot of us think we are incredibly strong on our own. We think we can handle everything that comes at us alone. We do not want to bother other people with our problems or our sadness and fears. We do not want to be a burden to others.

But perhaps we are not meant to go through everything alone. If someone extends their hand to help us, maybe we are supposed to take it. Everything happens for a reason, so if someone is offering to assist, perhaps we are meant to swallow our pride and allow ourselves to receive the help.

There is no shame in asking for or accepting assistance from another. Pride sometimes gets in our way though. We want to be the strong lion all the time rather than the wounded prey. But as strong as we are, we cannot be that strong a hundred percent of the time. It is just not possible.

But through our weakest moments, we learn so much about ourselves and others. We learn about compassion from the people around us. We learn trust and trustworthiness. We learn that asking for or accepting help does not make us weak, because there is strength in asking and accepting. You are not giving away your power, but sharing your power with someone else for the moment. You are not a burden. You are love!

Sending love and light!!

INNER FOCUS BEFORE OUTER FOCUS

Today's lesson of the day is about helping ourselves before we can help others. The guides have an analogy that really rings true here: when you are in an airplane, and the oxygen masks come down, are you instructed to help your child put their mask on first or are you supposed to put your mask on before them?

The answer is always put your own mask on first before you help someone else. If you lose oxygen, you are not going to be able to help anyone else. So, we must help ourselves first so that we can be of service to others in need. How does this example translate into our day to day lives?

Sometimes we find ourselves focusing on others to dissociate from our own problems. To us they are healthy distractions since we are assisting others. Helping people gives us a wonderful feeling, but it is only a temporary band-aid over the deep cuts of the past.

It is time to seek help to heal those deeper wounds. A band-aid will only work for so long before it will need to be replaced repeatedly. Those deep cuts need to be healed from the inside out. Once you get the help you need, you will love yourself again and find a strong inner strength, your energy frequency will rise, and then you will be able to share your strength and love with others. Your healing journey begins today!! You got this, warrior!!

Sending love and light!!

CALMNESS THROUGH STRUGGLES

Today's lesson of the day is about staying calm during a creativity struggle. You have this amazing idea. In fact, you have already started it. Perhaps you are even halfway through a project already, and now you are drawing a blank.

This happens to everyone. And it always seems to happen when we are on a roll. We start with so much steam that it can get very frustrating when you come to a crossroads and you are not sure what to do. This is a moment for you to stop pulling your hair out. Feeling frustrated will only make you feel less and less creative and confident.

This is the time to put the project away for a moment. Step away so that you can get a clear head. When you move away from a frustrating situation, and you give your mind a chance to settle, the ideas will eventually start to flow again. This is a time to not be discouraged. Instead, go for a walk in nature, meditate, get to a calm place. Inspiration is everywhere all around us! And soon you will see you have the upper hand, and you will be able to carry on in no time.

The creative process takes time and should not be rushed. And feeling blocked is something that happens in life. Do not give it negative energy because you do not deserve that. Take some breaths, step aside, and your creativity will flow again! Perhaps even stronger than before!

Sending love and light!!

THINK BEFORE YOU ACT

Today's lesson of the day is about thinking before we act. Sometimes we are so anxious about getting something done that we leap before we look in front of us. We make decisions based on our egos rather than what is best for us. Our egos are very powerful human parts of us that will always be there. Our egos make us feel anxious, impatient, fearful, doubtful, all the negative emotions that are put in place to protect us when we are in real danger.

But you are currently not in real immediate danger at this very moment, so your ego needs to be set aside. Fighting or flighting is not necessary right now. Before you go straight into fast action, pause, take some deep breaths, and sit with yourself for a few moments. It is time to listen to your intuition. Your intuition is like a best friend telling you what to do. And it is correct one hundred percent of the time.

You do not need to act so fast. The right answers will come along. Close your eyes and consider the possibilities. The answer will come to you, and then you can make your move. Taking long, deep breaths can really be a powerful thing. Just closing your eyes and taking three long, deep breaths can ground you again and help to clear the fog a bit. And who does not need some grounding?

Sending love and light!!

TRUST THIS NEW PATH

Today's lesson of the day is to trust the new work path you are going to begin or have just begun! It has been a long road. You have been going from one job to another, unsure of your future or the direction. You feel like you have recently been walking through life without any clarity. What is it I am supposed to be doing? Why is everything working out the way it is?

Remember that life is about the journey, not the end result. We always want to get to the finish line when life is about the process and progress. Now you have a new job opportunity, and you have either started it or going to start it soon, and you are uncertain about everything. Perhaps you thought your life by now would be one way and now it has gone in a completely new direction.

But remember that everything in this world is happening *for* us not *to* us. That is very important. You are exactly where you are meant to be at this very moment. Do not fight the journey because life is going to keep moving forward regardless if you want to hit the pause button.

What can you learn from this new opportunity? What new opportunities can come from it? If everything happens for a reason, what positive thing is this leading you towards? What is this teaching you? Trust in your path even when you are uncertain or confused. You will soon have clarity.

Sending love and light!!

RELEASING BURDEN

Today's lesson of the day is about releasing the burden you have been carrying for so long. We often have issues that weigh us down on a daily basis. Either we have gone through a traumatic event recently or we have fears that stop us from fully living. Perhaps you are waiting for medical advice or results or you are waiting for a job offer that has not come yet. Perhaps you were rude to a friend or family member and you cannot stop thinking about it.

There are many things that can burden us, but please know that this burden is short lived. Nothing lasts forever. You may not feel you are on solid ground at the moment, but you are nearing the shore. So, for now, take a pause and take some deep breaths to ground yourself. This will help your anxiety to dissipate a bit. Some of our burdens will end by themselves with time, and some of our burdens we have the power to release ourselves.

If this burden is one you created, it is time to make amends and make things right. Take this heavy weight off your shoulders. This negative energy is not doing you any favors. If this is a burden you did not create and was placed on you such as awaiting job offers, medical test results, etc., know that this is short lived, and this feeling of anxiety and heaviness is coming to an end. You got this!!

Sending love and light!!

OBSERVE THE ROADBLOCKS

Today's lesson of the day is when you feel life keeps knocking you down, take a moment to understand why. There are moments in all of our lives where life keeps handing us one negative thing after another. And sometimes it just feels like bullets are hitting us from every angle. It is at these times that we need to step aside for a moment and get some clarity.

No matter how much you try to do good in the world, you keep hitting roadblock after roadblock. Your path seems confusing and more difficult than ever before. Perhaps you have already been through enough negativity, and you do not understand why the bad things keep coming into your life.

One of the most difficult things to remember is that everything is happening for us not to us. Perhaps you are being pushed in another direction, but you are fighting it. Perhaps you are being protected by being forced to go down a new path. Maybe you are not meant to get that job because it would have been a nightmare. Perhaps you were not meant to get that surgery at this time because it was not time yet. Perhaps you lost a friend recently due to a disagreement, but they did not really care about you to begin with.

This is a time to pause and reflect. Instead of going into the negative, go into: how could this be working *for* me? Sometimes asking this question can suddenly give you clarity and a sense of calm. There is always a plan for us, and it is during these moments we must trust the process the most, even though it sometimes feels impossible to do it. You got this, warrior!

Sending love and light!!

HOLIDAY NOSTALGIA

Today's lesson of the day is to bring nostalgia back to holidays year-round. When holidays approach, and every year we get older, we feel further removed from those magical moments we had as children. The fireplace lit and sparkling, the holiday decorations up as a constant reminder of the magic, trick or treating, pumpkin farms, the gatherings your family had, the joy of the different seasons warming your heart, the love and laughter.

Life is hard. It is not meant to be easy. So, we need to bring in joy and bliss as much as we possibly can. We can create those moments for ourselves so that we can turn the ordinary into the extraordinary. Bring the blissful and joyful moments back.

Play holiday music throughout your house that makes you giddy. Watch movies that put you in the mood. Throw a party with your friends and family. Throw a few! Have a potluck so it is not so expensive! It is about the power of community than anything else. Put up some decorations that make you smile.

All holidays are a perfect time where we can find the fun and lightness during difficult moments. Where time stops and the only thing that matters is that very moment. Where we can forget about our troubles even for a second. Where even if we have lost so much, there is still so much to be grateful for each day! Make all holidays as beautiful as you are!

Sending love and light!!

SAVING MONEY

Today's lesson is to save money so that you can do things you have always wanted to do! You have been thinking for quite some time that you need to get out of here for a while. What place have you always dreamed of going? Maybe you have always wanted to buy a house. Perhaps there is something you have always wanted to do or buy that is very expensive.

It is time to start saving that money so that you can make your dreams come true. It is time to set some money aside every month for your dreams. Perhaps it is in a separate bank account labeled "Dreams." Perhaps it is hidden in your house, so it is nearby. Wherever you want to keep it. Maybe it is $100 a month. That adds up very quickly over a short period of time!

Our dreams seem out of reach sometimes because we think about the big number we need to get to in order to make our dreams happen. And that number can feel overwhelming and daunting and impossible. But remember that nothing is impossible. If you break down that number over a series of months, suddenly it is much more manageable, and your dreams no longer seem out of reach!

Start collecting for your big dream vacations or your dream weddings or your dream creations or whatever it is today, and make your dreams a beautiful reality! Nothing is impossible if you break it down into smaller pieces. Consider each addition to your dream stash as an accomplishment, because it is!! It is all about the journey.

Sending love and light!!

THE BRAGGART

Today's lesson of the day is not to brag about all the amazing things you have in life when someone else next to you may not. It is one thing to be excited about something new that has come into your life that brings you joy, and you want to share that joy with others; it is an entirely different thing when you gloat and bring others down through your own happiness.

Maybe someone next to you does not have the family life that you do. Maybe the person next to you can only dream about financial security at this moment and prays every day for help, when you have an abundance of wealth. Maybe the person next to you struggles to find transportation, when you have three cars. Maybe someone next to you is always hitting roadblock after roadblock, and you are having a life that is much easier.

This is not the time to throw your abundance of monetary joys in someone else's face. In fact, it is never the time to do that. Luck has nothing to do with your life path when your path has been planned out by you from before you were born. There is a reason you have been given all the great wealth you have been given, the family you have created, the life that you are leading. This is the time to have that realization now.

If you are fortunate to have the wealth you do, it is time to help others in need. If you are fortunate to have that big family, teach your children to be honest, giving, and loving beings. You have been given a very important responsibility. This was not luck that you have what you have. Everything is a lesson. A lesson in helping others less fortunate rather than bragging about it. You have the power to start making a positive difference today. It is time.

Sending love and light!!

SEPARATE JOURNEYS

Today's lesson of the day is when you feel you have nothing; this is the time to change your mindset and see the truth. Recently you have been feeling down on yourself. You look at others in your life and see how they are living, how they are loving, how they are enjoying. And it makes you feel like your life is not good enough. "How come I do not have these things?"

But we are all on our own separate journeys. We could literally look at anyone's life and find something we do not have. Maybe you know someone who is always vacationing somewhere. Maybe you know someone who has always had a stable and secure job. Maybe you know someone who has been happily married for many years. Comparing yourself to others will only make you feel less than in some way.

The truth is you have something all those people do not. And perhaps other people are envious of you because of it. It is time to change your mindset from what you do not have to what you do have. Perhaps you are brilliantly creative! Perhaps you have terrific health! Perhaps you have great friends in your life or you are close to your family!

Not everyone has what you have. So, today is the day to start recognizing that. Sit down and make a positive list of everything you have in your life. Everything from your friend and family list to having a roof over your head to your health to even your growth over the years as a human being. Now read that list every day. See your abundance of positivity in front of you. Positivity will make you a much happier and fulfilled person. The energy we choose is a powerful thing!

Sending love and light!!!

WALKING AWAY FROM RELATIONSHIPS

Today's lesson of the day is about walking away from relationships that are not serving you. This can be a love relationship, a friendship, or even a business partnership. In these situations, you are finding that you are doing all the work. You may even have people telling you, as observers, that without you putting in all that effort, that relationship would not even exist.

As they say, "it takes two to tango." And it is true. You could try to lead, but if the other person is not even moving, then why bother? Relationships of all kinds are a lot of work. It takes trust and commitment to keep it going. You may find the person never contacts you, that you have to be the one to initiate conversations all the time.

In a relationship, you may find that you are always the one pursuing the other, but if you stopped pursuing one day the relationship would fizzle out quickly. If it is a business partnership, you may find yourself feeling overwhelmed and frustrated because you are having to do things alone while your partner is nowhere to be found.

You can absolutely have a conversation about it with the other person, that is always a good way to start. But if a conversation does not work, it is time to take your power back and make the decision to walk away. These types of relationships, once addressed, do not get better. The other person is just not as "all in" as you are. And you deserve to have someone who is as equally committed to the relationship. Because you are worth it!

Sending love and light!!

STARTING OVER

Today's lesson of the day is about starting over after losing everything. You have been through an absolute whirlwind of emotional trauma. You find yourself in a place where you have hit rock bottom. You may have lost a relationship, had to move abruptly, are forced to be separated from your loved ones, or struggling with an addiction. You feel like your life is over. How are you supposed to recover from this?

It is time to take a pause for a moment because you are spiraling into a very dark place of negative energy. Yes, we need to feel all the feels that are flowing through us; grieve the life you have lost. But there needs to be a moment, after the grieving process, that you need to pull yourself out of the darkness. Staying in a negative place will only cause you more harm by bringing other negative energies to you. You do not deserve that.

It is time to realize that this is the beginning of a new chapter. The pain caused in the previous chapter has ended and you are safe again. This new chapter is about emotional healing. It is time to take the steps to stop the spiraling and start to climb the ladder back up to the light. If you look up from the deep and dark hole you are in, the light can be seen no matter how far away it looks. The light is never gone.

What are the steps you will take today? Decide to take the first step of getting out of bed in the morning. Maybe you decide to get dressed. Take a walk in nature barefoot to let the Earth's energy fill you or sit and meditate. For additional help, therapy and group work are always options as well. You are not alone. You will succeed because you will slowly start to change your energy frequency. And you will climb that ladder one minute, one day, one week at a time as you continue to heal. You will finally find relief.

Sending love and light!!

THE BULLIES

Today's lesson of the day is how to deal with the bullies. There are people out there who are jealous of you. Jealous of your kindness, jealous of your generosity, jealous of your ability to help others, jealous of your many talents and accomplishments. Jealousy causes people to behave in ways they never thought possible. But for some reason you have become the target. In these situations, it is important to dissect why the person is acting the way they are. There is always a root cause. Usually when a bully strikes, it is to protect themselves from their own misery.

Bullies survive on reaction. That means your power is not to react to them at all. They simply no longer exist in your world. Completely shut them out of your life. Do not listen to their words, do not acknowledge them, do not pay attention to them because they are not worth it. If it is someone of authority, you have a choice to leave that toxic situation.

If you stop "feeding" them, they will have no choice but to move on. Standing up for yourself is not allowing the vampire in. If it is multiple people at work, it may be time to walk away. They succeed when you react, get upset, or fight back. We cannot control others, but we can control ourselves. Always choose to stay in the highest energy frequency. Not doing so only causes you harm, and you do not need that in your life. Never think of your kindness as weakness, because kindness is your strength!

Also, to protect yourself: Every morning when you wake up, close your eyes and imagine you are surrounded by a reflective mirror of protection. Imagine only positive energy coming through and negative energy bouncing off back to the person. Really imagine this protective mirror shield of positive energy, believe it wholeheartedly, and say out loud that it will last all day. You will be protected.

Sending love and light!!

YOU ARE A POWERFUL BEING

Today's lesson of the day is knowing that you are a powerful being that is capable of manifesting what you want. The first thing to understand is that our souls are not in our physical bodies; our physical bodies are in our souls. Our souls are so much greater and larger than us. Only a small part of our souls are here having this "simulated" experience to learn and grow. We always have one foot here on Earth and the other foot in the spirit realm at all times. This means we have so much more power than you can imagine. We are manifesting this experience here on a daily basis, whether you know it or not, we choose everything. Almost like a video game in a way. We choose the character, we choose what we are fighting for, and we play it out. We are the players playing the game. We have the controls.

The universe is a very giving place where it will give you the experience you are desiring at any given moment. For example, if you fully believe your life is miserable the universe will gladly give you the experience of misery. Same goes for positivity. If you fully believe that your life is going the way it should and that everything is a positive lesson, the universe will give you that experience. It is not about punishment or judgement. It is about asking and receiving.

Now that you know your very real powers of manifestation, what will you do with this power? Choose to make things happen for yourself. There will always be negative things in our lives. That is part of the game. But it is how you react to it that matters. Always lead with love and compassion. Manifest the beautiful life you deserve!

Sending love and light!!!

TIME FOR A DECISION

Today's lesson of the day is to make a decision that has been weighing heavily on your shoulders for quite some time. You have been struggling lately with deciding about something very important, and it has been a burden that has caused you a lot of stress and anxiety. However, you are afraid of making the wrong choice.

It is time to weigh the possibilities. Take a deep breath and ground yourself. Get to a place of calm whether that means breathing exercises or meditation. It is impossible to make an important decision when your mind is racing. Breathing deeply and closing your eyes can help to ground yourself. Now make a list with all possible outcomes in regard to your decision you need to make. What are the pros and cons of each decision individually?

Look at your lists. Which option has more pros than cons? Which decision is going to bring you more peace, joy, and positive energy? Many times, deep down, we already know the answer to this question before we even make a list. But this helps to solidify the answers for us. Our intuition is always right a hundred percent of the time, but doing the exercise above with the lists will help you to start trusting yourself more in the future.

Even after reading this lesson, you may already know the answer to the question you are struggling with. If that is the case, know it is time to release that burden from your shoulders. Life is heavy and can feel like a thousand bricks on top of you. It is time to start removing the bricks one by one so that you can live freely. Always lead with compassion and love and the answer will come to you.

Sending love and light!!

TAKING AND TAKING

Today's lesson of the day is to realize when you have been taking and taking from others without giving anything back in return. It is time to look deep into your relationships with your partners, family, and friends. As much as we would like to think we have equality in our relationships in regard to giving and taking, it is not always the case.

It is not easy to evaluate ourselves in our relationships. We always like to think we are always giving a hundred percent. But are we really? Are we making as much of an effort as we think we are? Perhaps you are giving your all to a few of your relationships (i.e. partnerships, family, friends), but possibly neglecting others. This is not judgement, this is just reality. It is not an easy thing to do. But this is the time to be mindful of it.

Go through the important people in your life one by one. Which relationships do you notice others making the effort but you not so much? Be honest with yourself. Are they contacting you but you rarely, if ever, contact them? Maybe it is only one person you know that this is true for. Really evaluate the relationship in your mind. Evaluate yourself always with love, kindness, and grace. Do not beat yourself down over it. Just acknowledge the fact that you have not put in an equal effort.

Now it is time to change that. Pick up the phone and give that person a call today. Plan an evening to get together! If the person really means that much to you, make the effort to be in their lives just as much as the other person does to be in yours. Give and take. Show the other person that you appreciate them. You will be glad that you did!

Sending love and light!!

THE CLEANUP

Today's lesson of the day is to stop cleaning up other people's messes. We all want peace and harmony, and we all want others to have it as well. But what if you are constantly doing all the work for others because they will not do it for themselves? What lessons are those people learning? If you are doing everything for another person who is more than capable of completing a task on their own all the time, is it being more helpful or harmful to the other?

We are all on our own separate journeys, and all our journeys intertwine while we are here. We do not like to see others struggling so we have a natural want to help in any way we can to lessen someone else's load. Helping others is a beautiful thing, and everyone should continue to do that. But what happens when you start noticing a pattern that not only are you cleaning up their problems once or a few times, but you are trying to get them out of trouble constantly?

You will start to get a feeling in the pit of your stomach that says: Wait a minute, why am I having to do this again? Why aren't they doing things for themselves? Are they purposefully taking advantage of me? These questions are valid. You are now interfering with that person's life journey. They are clearly meant to learn some difficult lessons in life to help their soul grow, but how can they learn those lessons if you are doing all the hard work for them?

If you are noticing this pattern, you are agreeing with this and nodding your head. You know that you can no longer pick up after this person. It is time for them to learn the hard lesson of responsibility. As difficult as it sounds, you need to let them learn on their own. You cannot protect them from their own mistakes or their lack of trying. It is time to release that burden and continue on your own journey. Release their burden from your shoulders.

Sending love and light!!

CHERISH LOVED ONES

Today's lesson of the day is about cherishing those you love in your life. You have so many people in your life who have been there for you from the beginning. Without even asking they have been by your side and have given you support, defended you, and given you endless amounts of joy. It is time to turn around and show your loved ones how much you appreciate them.

Our minds immediately go to monetary gifts, but that is not what this lesson is about. Show them by telling them you love them. Make them dinner. Show them support. Defend their honor if someone is talking badly about them. Always let your loved ones know how much you care. Because you are extremely blessed with such incredible people around you.

But this is not a coincidence. You have known many of these same people before in other lifetimes. You travel back in groups to find each other again whether they be family members, romantic relationships, and friendships. You feel like you have known them all your life because you have known them for much longer than you can imagine. Your relationship just clicks almost like you are starting right where you left off.

Celebrate the reunion. You, souls, have all been through so much together, and you have found each other once again! Celebrate your close relationships because they go much deeper than you could ever imagine! And how amazing is it that you are traveling with a group of amazing souls through each life experience? It shows we have never been and never will be alone here, and that is an extremely comforting thought!

Sending love and light!!

IN AND OUT

Today's lesson of the day is understanding why certain people come into your life and out of your life at different times. You have noticed that one day you have a best friend that you see almost every day for years. Or you are in a relationship that has lasted a long time. Then suddenly, almost out of nowhere, that person or persons almost disappear(s) from your life as though they were never there to begin with.

This lesson is all about energy frequency. Always remember that like attracts like. Positive energy will always attract energy of the same frequency. Same with negative energy. So, why did these people fall off the face of the planet? How were you so close at one point of your life, and then suddenly nonexistent the next? How is any of that possible?

Your energy frequency shifted. You either raised or lowered your frequency and your frequency with the other person no longer matched up. When this occurs, it is challenging to keep the relationship going because you are no longer on the same wavelength. For example: either they were too negative energetically and you became a much more positive person, or you became more pessimistic and they became more optimistic in their life.

This is why people come and go from your life seemingly out of nowhere. But it is not out of nowhere, and it is not a coincidence. They were meant to be in your life for a specific period until they were not. If you force the relationship to continue, you will find that you constantly feel a disconnect, and that will only become more of a struggle for you. It is time to reflect on why those relationships faded into the past, and then be more present in the now.

Sending love and light!!

THE FEAR OF LOSS

Today's lesson of the day is now that you have gotten everything you have ever wanted, you need to stop fearing losing it all. Maybe you have just received a clean bill of health. Maybe you have gotten the job you have always wanted. Maybe you have met the person of your dreams. Maybe you have come into some money. Now that you have gotten what you have wished for, your ego is creeping in, making you think that this happiness is only temporary.

We always wish for the best for ourselves and then once we get it, we start putting negative energy towards them. "Well, now that I met this amazing person, there has got to be something wrong with them" or "I am finally free of this illness, but it is just my luck that it will come back" or "It was a slim chance that I got this job, nothing good lasts forever. It is only a matter of time." We begin putting negative thoughts and energy towards the things we love in life.

Our egos love to make us doubt and fear and have anxiety over what brings us joy. Instead of living in the moment, we are already living in a negative future that we have created in our minds. We are worried about everything and not living. We are self-sabotaging ourselves. It is important to remember the law of attraction. Positive energy attracts positive energy and so on. So, since this is the case, what you are putting out into the universe really does matter.

Make sure to toss your ego aside. You deserve the amazing things coming to you! Keep positive energy around you and within you at all times, and the universe will give you positive energy in return. We cannot control what happens around us, but we can control ourselves and how we react. Look around you, see the abundance of joy that is in your life, and just allow yourself to be happy without the doubt and anxiety.

Sending love and light!!

ON THE DEFENSE

Today's lesson of the day is to not be on the defense with new people in your life before getting to know them. You have been burned before by people around you. You feel others have let you down more often than not. So, when you meet someone new, you already have a negative, preconceived notion about them. You judge them harshly from the beginning because who have you really been able to trust?

This is not about the person you have met at all, rather you have your own defenses up from your past. Not everyone is the same as others you have known, and this new person you have met could be different. If you put your anger from your past onto someone you do not even know, you have already dismissed them without knowing what could have been. You are already creating a negative future before it has even begun. The thing is, you could be dismissing someone great for you.

It is time to heal the wounds of the past so that you can become more trusting in your present. You have built so many walls up you cannot see over them. You would rather be isolated than give someone a chance. Dealing with the reasons why will help to free you from yourself. The walls you have built to protect you are now harming you, hindering you from making a new positive connection.

Getting to the root of the issue is important so that you can finally trust again. It is not healthy to be in fight or flight mode all the time, and this will be a first step into moving towards a healthier future. And if you know the root issue(s), you need to start the process of healing those past wounds whether that is with therapy, talking with a friend, or journaling. Self-reflection is an extremely powerful tool. You will begin to trust again, but it is time to break down those high walls you have built first.

Sending love and light!!

RAISE YOUR ENERGY

Today's lesson of the day is to focus on raising your energy frequency so that amazing things happen naturally for you rather than by force. Human beings are always frantically chasing something. Maybe it is a dream, maybe it is money, maybe it is a relationship. But frantically, desperately chasing after something, without you realizing it, is actually lowering your energy frequency. Desperation and fear will drag you down very fast.

But the lowering of energy does not stop there. What happens when you get what you have been desperately chasing after? You have to fight to keep it. That equals stress and anxiety and depression which lowers your energy frequency even further. This is an energy trap. What is meant to make you happy, does the exact opposite, because you are always living in constant fear. And you will feel that you are in constant misery and anxiety over it.

So, instead of chasing after things frantically, focus on the energy that is flowing out of you. Do things that make you happy, your frequency will raise. Be with people who bring you joy and laughter, your frequency will raise. Go to work at a job that makes you feel excited, energized, and fulfilled, your frequency will raise. Love yourself fully, your frequency will raise. Remove yourself from toxic people and toxic environments, and your frequency will raise.

What will occur is you will be living without fear, doubt, and negativity making your soul expand positively. You will notice you no longer need to chase anything because positive things will be attracted to you. People will be drawn to the energy you are giving off. It is time to focus on raising your energy frequency, and everything else will fall into place. Trust.

Sending love and light!!

GIVING TO THOSE IN NEED

Today's lesson of the day is to give to others in need because you have been there, and understand what it is like. In the past you have felt down and out. You asked people for help, and you received the love and kindness from others. And from this difficult time in your life, you were able to rise above and shine brightly. You have established yourself. You have stability. You have the confidence and security you always wished you had.

Remember, though, you did not get where you are alone. You were fortunate enough to have help from others whether they were family, friends, coworkers, or even strangers who were wanting to help. Sometimes it takes a village. How amazing was it to feel that love from people who were rooting for you? Do not ever forget what that felt like.

But now it is time to remember how fortunate you were, and it is time to look around you to those who are less fortunate. They are exactly where you were at your most challenging moments. It is time to reach out your hand to help and assist the way others helped you in the past. Showing that love for another human being is one of the most beautiful acts. Especially when you are not expecting anything in return.

We are all in different stages of our lives at the human and soul level, and we must remember that we are all one, large community. We all came from the same place. Helping others without personal gain is a high energy frequency. You may not gain something monetarily from it, but you will get something far greater: the beautiful growth of your soul. And nothing is greater than that because that is the reason we are all here in the first place: to love and grow.

Sending love and light!!

YOUR OWN ADDICTIONS

Today's lesson of the day is about the effect that addictions have on the people closest to you. No matter what you are addicted to, you have noticed that people are beginning to or already have distanced themselves. You feel like they have abandoned you and you cannot understand why. You may not even believe you have a problem, but others seem to keep trying to tell you that you do.

When someone has an addiction of any kind, people who are closest to you are always going to try and help. They are going to nudge you to get the help you need no matter how uncomfortable it is to bring up. But the rest of the work is up to you. You have to want to get help for yourself and you must first understand that you have an addiction in the first place.

However, once those loved ones try to intervene and help you, and you refuse to help yourself, that is when you will start to notice those people start to drift away from you. It is not because they do not love you, it is because of three things that are occurring: they cannot stand to see you harming yourself, you are on different energy frequencies, or they are protecting their own energy.

This is to understand why people are distancing themselves from you at this time. However, you have the power to turn this around. You have a choice to make. Always choose to have a higher energy frequency so that you can have the beautiful life you deserve. If this addiction stems from trauma, you know it is time to get the help you need so that you can truly move forward. The decision is yours. It is time to face this head-on.

Sending love and light!!

TRUST THE DIRECTION

Today's lesson of the day is to trust that you are headed in the right direction, and that you will be able to celebrate very soon!! You have felt a bit lost for a while now. As though you are on a boat you are rowing, and the land seems far away still. But this is your reminder that you are on your right path. You are exactly where you are supposed to be at this exact moment in time. It is time to trust the process, and trust that there is a plan for you because there is always a plan.

Our life paths are a big mystery. People think they know their path, and then they suddenly hit a brick wall; they are forced to go down a completely different path they never imagined for themselves. Perhaps, in your mind, you were always meant to be a professional singer, and suddenly you find yourself opening a bakery. Or you have never known what your life path was and now you are finally understanding later in life.

What you need to remember is the journey is the most important part of this whole experience here. You needed to go through everything in your life positive or negative to get to where you needed to go today. There are important lessons in everything. Look back at your life and notice the twists and turns. You will see a pattern and a reasoning for everything if you look hard enough. Just know that you are on the right path regardless and everything will become clear to you very soon.

We are always being guided every day, and we need to trust the process as difficult as that can be most times. You are nearing the shore now, and you will be able to celebrate soon! You will have that clarity you have been hoping for. Trust the process.

Sending love and light!!

OPENING UP AND EXPLORATION

Today's lesson of the day is to start exploring your intuitive gifts. We all have them. These special powers we all have within us are meant to be discovered and utilized in our lives. It is our birthright. So, now it is time to consider what your abilities are and be open to exploring them. People always talk about wishing they had superpowers when they already have them.

What kind of superpowers do you have? Maybe you have dreams or premonitions of things that happen in the future that you cannot explain. Maybe you can see or hear things that others are not attuned to. Maybe you feel drawn to spirituality because you are remembering that there is much more to our lives than just here in "Earth school." Some people remember these abilities at a very young age, and some have their spiritual awakening much later in life.

These intuitive abilities have always been within you. So, the question is: why are some more in tuned to these special gifts than others? If you are reading this saying: I do not have any "powers." This is not true. This is all due to energy frequency. If you are living in a lower frequency, you are most likely always leaning more on ego than your intuition. Ego is our doubts, our fears, our human traits. When we lean into ego, we may actually notice these gifts, but we judge them and call them coincidence.

It is time to lean into your abilities. To remember who we really are outside of these physical bodies. We are incredibly strong, powerful beings. It is time to step into our power and share it with others. These gifts are not something to fear, they are beautiful! Open yourself up to what is rightfully yours, and you will see magical things happen!

Sending love and light!!

GIVING OTHERS STRENGTH

Today's lesson of the day is about giving others strength when they are not strong for themselves. Life throws a lot at us all at once, and even though life only throws at us what we can handle, sometimes it feels impossible still. Everyone knows how it feels to be in that position because we all have been there many times before. It is time to look around you and see those who may need a boost of your strength.

You may see someone down and out who needs a positivity boost, or if someone is struggling with their job, or just struggling in general. Today is the day to reach out to that person so they know that they are not alone. Just a few kind words can really help someone. More than you could imagine.

The person may feel stuck, and you can be there to offer some solutions to show them there are possibilities. If they are having relationship struggles, offer a listening ear so they can get it off their chest. You may even have some great advice for them because you have been through it yourself!

It is about being there and giving support to someone else who needs it. Whether they decide to take your advice does not really matter in the long run. It is their own journey, and they will ultimately decide. But it is the thought here that counts. Being there to lift someone up when they cannot quite get there themselves. Always lead with love, compassion, and understanding. That will go a very long way!!

Sending love and light!!

BELIEVING IN YOURSELF

Today's lesson of the day is about believing in yourself completely because a new job opportunity is coming, and you will be able to celebrate soon!! You have been searching for a job for a while now, and you have started to wonder if anything is out there. You have interviewed multiple times and everything seems to be at a standstill. It is time to throw those positive thoughts into the universe.

Did you know that the thoughts you think actually matter? We are much more powerful beings than you think. Everything is energy. We are energy, animals are energy, plants are energy, tables and chairs are energy. Even our thoughts are energy. Everything is made up of energy. So, why does energy matter, and why talk about this at all? Because energy is everything and everywhere. If you put out negative or uncertain thoughts, you will attract the same energy back that you are putting out into the universe.

If you believe you are incapable of doing something or have any doubts at all, it will be so because you say it is so. This is a time to manifest what you want. You need to fully believe that you are going to get that great job you have been looking for. You need to believe it deep in your soul. The moment you start to think thoughts of self-doubt, self-deprecation, and fear, that is the energy you are putting out into the universe. You are basically asking the universe for the same energy you are giving. And who wants that?

The job you want is yours for the taking, so it is time to change your energy frequency to a positive one. No more feeling unworthy or down in the dumps. No more feeling sorry for yourself. Because you are worthy. You are enough. You are smart. You are talented. You are ready. Believe it wholeheartedly. You will get the job. You will find what you are looking for. Trust. If you believe it to be so, then it will be so.

Sending love and light!!

MANIFESTING RELATIONSHIPS

Today's lesson of the day is about manifesting a new beautiful relationship. You have been single for a while, and you are now ready for a new adventure with another person. Now it is time to consider a few important things first before diving head first into this new beautiful journey!

Energy frequency always seems to be brought up in these situations time and time again, but it is so important to understand that energy frequencies matter in every situation. For example, are you in a position in your life mentally and emotionally to be able to fully commit to another person? Are you over a past relationship that may have ended badly? Do you *need* someone in your life or *want* someone in your life? Do you love yourself fully and unconditionally?

If you have answered one or more of the questions above with an uncertain or negative answer, you are most likely not as ready as you hoped. We must be committed to ourselves first before jumping into something with another person. Remember that energy frequency attracts a frequency of the same wavelength. If you are feeling unhappy in your life and miserable, or if you do not love yourself fully, you will attract someone who will be of that same frequency.

However, if you have answered the questions above with positivity, excitement, and openness, then you are ready to manifest the person you have been dreaming about! Believe and imagine your new connection, that they are everything you could ever want in a person. It will take effort, so be vulnerable and put yourself out there. You will meet someone when the time is right.

Sending love and light!!

HEALING PAST TRAUMAS

Today's lesson of the day is about healing past trauma so that you can move forward into a future with endless possibilities. We have all been through some very difficult and traumatic times in our lives. Often, we take those moments and hide them away out of sadness, anxiety, depression, doubt, or fear. We do not want to deal with those moments because they are painful, and sometimes it is much easier to shove them away inside rather than facing our traumas head on so we can fully heal and move forward.

It was hard enough to go through the experience that gave us those traumatic moments let alone having to dig them back up and deal with them again. But we must. Nothing stays hidden away forever. The skeletons underneath will eventually come back to the surface. These skeletons can affect our future relationships, our work, and our lives.

168

With these negative energies festering inside, it will cause a chain of negative events to happen which is the opposite of what you deserve. However, you are an extremely strong person. You are much stronger than you think. So, it is time to get the help you need and face those traumatic moments head on so that you can see the incredible possibilities that are out there.

You are currently in a fog, but no fog lasts forever! It is time for that fog to lift. Face those traumas, not with fear and anger and negativity, but with love and compassion for yourself. Once you can remove the fog, you will see that anything and everything is possible. You will be able to trust and love again. But more importantly, you will be able to love yourself. And that is the most important piece of the puzzle. Love yourself inside and out, unconditionally. This new journey begins today!!

Sending love and light!!

STOP THE FIGHTING

Today's lesson of the day is to stop fighting with your partner in a relationship. You have been fighting with your partner time and time again. Things are getting more vicious. The energy in the home is so thick that you could slice the air with a knife. This thickness is the negative energy. The kind of energy that others can feel when they walk into the home.

It is time to take a pause and to evaluate your lives individually here. To dig deep into why you are both always fighting, you need to go back to the beginning of when the fighting started. Ask why you ever allowed yourself to get to this point? It often occurs because of an event that created a deep wound, and old wounds are reopened. Remember that a relationship takes two. We must evaluate ourselves first and reflect. What was my part in this? How am I accountable? This is not judgement on yourself; this is taking responsibility for your part.

Once you have discovered your part and what started your anger towards your partner in the past, you need to find out if communication is the issue which is one of the biggest reasons, if there were red flags from the beginning that you ignored because you just wanted to be in the relationship that badly, if there is a possibility that you enjoy the drama in some way that you love fighting, and if this relationship is salvageable.

If you truly love each other, it is time to heal old and new wounds and move forward in a respectful manner for both parties either with counseling or on your own. You will need to work as a team. A team you both created for a reason originally. Rediscover why you are in each other's lives so the negative fog surrounding you can lift, and you can both live a much happier and fulfilled life!!

Sending love and light!

THE SAFETY OF YOUR INNER CHILD

Today's lesson of the day is about letting your inner child-self know that they are safe. When we go through major stages of life such as childhood, teen years, etc., those parts of you remain. The experiences you had during those times stay with us as well, and affect how we live in the present. Imagine your child-self still within. As we grew into adulthood, some of our childhood fears came with us.

It can be fear of judgement, fear of failure, fear of being treated badly, or not loving ourselves completely. It is time to have a heart-to-heart conversation with our child-selves. We need to tell our inner child that we love them and that they are safe. Checking in with ourselves to make sure we are okay. It does us no good if we are constantly thrown into chaotic situations or situations where we feel lost or out of control; we will just feel anxious, nervous, and scared. We need to ground ourselves.

Meditation is key here. Sit with yourself for a moment and visualize your inner child. Imagine you see them worried in a corner. What would you tell them to make them feel better? How can you ease their mind so that they are not so scared and anxious? Ask them why they are so afraid. What happened to make them feel that way? Does the situation you are in remind them of something that happened during childhood?

Once you understand where your inner child's fear and anxiety is coming from, tell them they are safe. Tell them that you love them unconditionally. Believe what you are saying. You will notice that you will start to feel calmer. It is about getting to know yourself, and knowing you have things under control. And you will manifest joy. Through safety, love, and security we find happiness, and that is always the goal. Happiness within ourselves.

Sending love and light!!

RECONNECTION FROM THE PAST

Today's lesson of the day is about reconnecting with a childhood friend because you have been thinking about them a lot lately. In life, friends come in and out of our lives frequently. At one point they are our best friends and the next they disappear from our lives. This is very normal because we have soul contracts with everyone in our lives.

A soul contract is a list of lessons and events you create with your spirit guides and light council to decide what you want to learn during this lifetime. Imagine that a soul contract is a script you have written in the spirit realm, and you are placed into a body of your choosing. You need other "actors" to help you play the certain parts as well. Therefore, everyone's story is interwoven with a purpose.

The reason this is important is once a soul helps us to learn the lesson we were meant to learn, they have done their part and they exit your stage. You suddenly feel a disconnection with them or a life change happens and the person seems to disappear. Remember the positive lessons those people taught you and how it helped you to progress. That was no coincidence because there are no coincidences. And now, after all these years, this person you were friends with is suddenly in your mind again.

Perhaps you are thinking about them again because they are thinking about you as well. If you feel the urge to contact that person, there is a reason. Remember that our intuition is never wrong, so if you feel that urge to reconnect, there is always a possibility that you are meant to after all these years. Something great could come from the reunion.

Sending love and light!!

MANIFESTING HEALTH

Today's lesson of the day is about manifesting great health in your future. We are powerful beings. Our thoughts, words, and actions matter because they all have energy attached. If everything has an energy connection, the more positive our thoughts, the more positive things will happen. This can be a challenging thing to do because we are used to living by our egos or our human traits which give us our doubts, fears, sadness, and anxiety.

However, we have control over our own thoughts, the words we say, and the actions we take in our lives. Every one of those things are choices. And because of the Law of Attraction, we need to choose wisely. The Law of Attraction is about the energies that we give off, and that the universe will give us the same energies back in return. This means we can manifest exactly what we want by our thoughts, words we speak, and our actions.

You have had some challenging moments health wise in your life. It is time to notice when these health issues began in your life. You will see that they often coincide with negative things occurring at once. Perhaps you are in a negative relationship that is draining you. Perhaps you are in a job that makes you miserable. Perhaps you do not love yourself fully. All these issues can then manifest in the physical body.

Your negative surroundings have caused harm, so now it is time to think about moving forward. Find ways to destress such as daily meditation. You need to get to a place of calm. Remove yourself from toxic environments or toxic people. Get to a positive place. Once you do you will notice your health will start to improve. We are always manifesting, so imagine incredible health for yourself. Stay in the highest energy frequencies such as love, humor, and laughter. You will see a change.

Sending love and light!!

ACCEPTING SUPPORT

Today's lesson of the day is about accepting support from others rather than isolating yourself during a difficult time. When something tragic or traumatic or difficult happens in our lives, we sometimes feel like hiding away. We feel embarrassed or we do not want to show anyone our weakness. But it is time to open yourself up to the people you love. Isolation only forces you to live in your emotions on repeat. It is time to stop torturing yourself.

Getting the negative emotions out of you will start to remove the emotional "sludge" from your body. Either talk to the people you love or a professional who can listen and give you advice. Whoever you are talking to, you will notice the more you talk about something, the lighter you will start to become. Negative energy is incredibly dense, and we feel weighted down and unable to move. It is time to remove that negative sludge and begin to heal.

Asking for support does not make you weak, acknowledging you need support makes you strong. As much as we would like to think we could do everything on our own, it shows strength when you can open up and start removing the negative energy within you. You do not deserve to be in that low negative energy frequency of sadness, depression, anxiety, anger, and fear. Removing these energies from your body is a type of protection. Because we do not want more negative energies to come to us and make our lives even more difficult.

Reach out to someone today. Show your strength that you have within you. Do not do this alone when you do not have to because there are always options. Asking for support is a much more positive energy than suffering in silence and isolation. Always choose the positive energy over the negative no matter how difficult it can be to do sometimes. Trust the process.

Sending love and light!!

A NEW CREATIVE
OPPORTUNITY

Today's lesson of the day is about a new creative opportunity that is coming your way, but needing patience. You have been hoping for this new opportunity for a while, and you are starting to believe it will never happen. It is something very creative such as art, design, music, or performance. It is a long time coming that sometimes it feels like you are on a boat that is ways away from shore, and all you need to do is get to land and you will finally get your chance.

This lesson is to remind you to keep your eye on the prize. It is not a time to feel doubtful or uncertain of yourself because the universe will give you that experience you are unknowingly asking for. Do not end up being your own barrier. Imagine in your head that you already have the opportunity you are seeking. See yourself doing it, and you will make it so.

The universe is always listening to us, so our thoughts really do matter each and every day. So, keep those positive thoughts coming. In your mind, tell yourself you already have the creative opportunity. You will notice your chance approaching much faster than before. No more doubting yourself. No more feeling down. Only say "it is happening *for* me!" And "my dreams *are* coming true." The universe will receive that energy and give you that experience.

However, know that if you do not receive something you really want at that specific time, you may be being protected by your spirit guides or higher-self because the opportunity could be the wrong one for you at that moment. So, keep believing in yourself and manifesting what you want, you will reach the shore soon enough. Trust the process. Have patience. Believe. The rest will take care of itself.

Sending love and light!

USING YOUR SKILLS TO CREATE

Today's lesson of the day is about using your skillsets to create a new financial opportunity. You have an idea of starting your own business. You do not have much passion for your current job, and you want something better. There are no coincidences. It is time to start writing out your new idea on paper and seeing if you can create this new opportunity. Everyone has something they can do well. What are your skillsets? Write them all down. If you are having a hard time with keeping your mind calm, meditation is a fantastic tool. Sit in stillness and let your spirit guides and higher-self guide you. Once you write them down, look at all the great things you have written. Now think of your favorite hobbies, the activities that you love doing so much that you cannot wait to do them because they bring you so much joy and happiness and fulfillment. Write them down.

With these lists, how can you serve humanity? It does not have to be on a large scale. Just helping others find their own joy and happiness in their lives. When we find our purpose in life, you will notice that everything fits into place. Life will always be challenging, but it should not be impossible. If what you are doing is feeling impossible and obstacles are constantly standing in your way, then your guides are telling you it is not your path. If you do not listen to them, they will keep putting obstacles in your way until you listen.

What is this amazing idea that you have? Make sure you love what it is and believe in it. If it is only about getting money, it will never work. There needs to be higher purpose that drives you. Intentions are energy. Keep those intentions positive and the universe will provide. Never doubt yourself and your abilities. You will see that anything is possible!! Trust.

Sending love and light!

TRUST THE NEGATIVE OBSTACLES

Today's lesson of the day is to trust your spirit guides when they throw negative obstacles in your way to get you back on your correct path. You already know your life path and purpose. But now that you have been in the business for many years, things seem to be falling apart around you. A job you had so much passion for is now causing you distress. You notice that toxic people and toxic environments are creeping into your work life more often. You feel so lost.

There are no coincidences in life, and everything happens for a reason. You are exactly where you are meant to be at this moment. Know that there is a plan. In fact, it is a plan of your own making that you created before you arrived here.

Our spirit guides' job is to keep us on the path we created for ourselves. They are like our stage managers of a production trying to make sure everything is going according to our script. Because we have free will, we sometimes do not listen to those little nudges from our guides to get us back on track. When this happens, you will notice negative things occurring in your life. You lose your job, your work environment is miserable, etc.

Life is supposed to be challenging but not impossible. If you are feeling this, your guides are trying to get you on the correct path. Take a pause. Meditate regularly. Listen to their guidance. Begin a journey of self-discovery. Your guides will lead you back to your path. When you are back on track, you will notice life seems a bit easier, and everything that is challenging will fall into place like the final piece to a puzzle. Trust the process.

Sending love and light!!

LOVING YOURSELF

Today's lesson of the day is about loving ourselves unconditionally. Before we are siblings, children of others, spouses, or parents, we are individuals first. It is time to look inward. During childhood, we often are taught the way to behave, be helpful, listen, and help others; however, somewhere in there we forgot about ourselves. We forget about who we are and forget how to love ourselves because there is too much interference.

From childhood, some become people pleasers, some feel their opinions do not matter, some hate things about themselves, some allow themselves to be manipulated, some learn they are not enough, etc. Our child-selves inside are feeling so incredibly lost and afraid, it is up to us to make sure they feel safe and loved unconditionally.

It is time to reintroduce yourself to yourself again. To remember who you are. It is time to stop listening to how others think you should be, and instead, love and embrace who you are right now. We have so much noise around us, so much negative fog floating in our minds. It is time to push that fog out and begin the process of loving ourselves. Look in the mirror. Look into your eyes and look deep into your soul. Look at your body vessel you chose for this life. Find the beauty in what you see.

We need to love everything about us inside and out, and that includes what you see as flaws. What you call "flaws" are beautiful. You chose this specific body when you came here. It is your vessel as you navigate through the world. Before we can truly love others fully, we must love ourselves. Once you do, you will be a beautiful force of positive energy, and you will be unstoppable!

Sending love and light!

FINDING THE BALANCE
AND CALM

Today's lesson is about working to find the balance and calm in your life. Chaos is all around us, and it can be a challenge to find the stillness. This is the moment when we must find even the shortest of moments to meditate and find the calm. In these moments, when things feel out of control, we cannot forget about ourselves. How can we help others if we are not grounded?

Meditation has been a practice for thousands of years, and there are so many benefits. On a non-spiritual level, meditation can reduce stress, help you find the calm, reduces anxiety, helps mind fog, can even help to reduce pain and inflammation. On a spiritual level, meditation helps you connect to your higher self and your guides. It can help you in discovering your true purpose here, and give you clarity.

It is all about setting an intention. Go into a meditation with a focus. Say to yourself or out loud, "I am meditating today to focus on opening my third eye" or "I am meditating today to remove my anxiety." Then close your eyes. Either sit in silence or play meditation music or do a guided meditation. Then, just be.

Do not worry if you are doing it correctly or not. There is no wrong or right way to meditate because it is a very personal experience. It is right for you because it feels right for you. Do not go into meditation with expectations. Just be. Some meditate for ten, fifteen, twenty minutes, some meditate for an hour to three or more hours. The more time the better. Do what fits into your schedule so that you can commit to this in your daily practice. You will begin noticing an incredible difference the more you do it. It will change your life. You got this, warrior!!

Sending love and light!!

SELF-JUDGEMENT

Today's lesson of the day is to stop judging ourselves. We are not perfect. That, in itself, is a relief! We have made many mistakes in the past, and we will continue to make mistakes in the future. And that is okay. How are we to learn and grow if we know everything? We cannot. Making mistakes or questionable choices is a part of this experience here on Earth. We do the best we can with the information we have at that particular time.

We may choose to be with someone who was never good for us from the beginning. We may choose a career based on our parents' wants and expectations rather than our own. We may have treated people poorly in the past. Whatever choices you have made, it does not have to dictate your future. Many times, when we look back on our lives and our decisions, we have so many regrets and we judge ourselves so harshly because of them.

The great thing about making negative or questionable decisions is that we can change our experience here at any time. Choose to be with someone who respects you. Go find your true calling and find your purpose. Start showing people kindness. Nothing in our lives is set in stone. You can be the person you want to be right now simply by flipping that switch on inside of you.

So, no more judging yourself. No more feeling down about your past decisions. We are constantly growing and learning and understanding. Instead of judging yourself, what have you learned from your experiences? Learning is positive energy. How can you take this information and make your life experience here better today? Those answers are very personal, and only you know them. It is time to start thinking about this now because you deserve to be happy! Start today!

Sending love and light!!

IT IS BETTER TO HAVE TRIED

Today's lesson of the day is it is better to have tried something and it not work out than never trying at all and having regrets. Trial and error is a part of life. It is how we know if we are on the right path or not. We have dreams as children, and we can either listen to our child-selves or we can ignore them. But what is worse? The fear of failure or the fear of regret?

The fear of failure is something we all deal with. What if something does not work out? Will this be a waste of time? What if I lose money on this? Is it too much of a risk? Do I really have the ability to accomplish this? We are always afraid of taking risks or making the wrong decisions. But life is about trial and error. It is about seeking the truth. Your truth. There will always be some fear that pushes through. It is our ego trying to protect us.

However, what if you never took any risks at all? What if you took a route that did not make you happy or fulfilled but was easier? True, sometimes taking the easier route can seem more appealing. Life can be hard enough as it is, and we do not want to complicate things further. We think of the words failure and disappointment and we allow those egoistic traits to guide us to safety. But when we do this, we eventually start having feelings of regret.

Regret haunts us more than if we tried something and it did not work out. In fact, often, when we try something that did not work, it often leads us to something else. Following your intuition will lead you to your life path and purpose. You can only succeed if you go for it. No one is going to knock on your door and hand you your purpose. A part of our life experience is discovering that for ourselves. No regrets. Trust the process.

Sending love and light!!

TRAUMA HEALING

Today's lesson of the day is about starting to heal from past traumas. We can find many times and events in our lives to be traumatizing. This can be anywhere from childhoods, intimate relationships, losing people in our lives, toxic environments, etc. Trauma is when we are heavily affected by our surroundings or events in a debilitatingly negative way.

We need to remember a key thing which is we cannot control other people around us. We cannot control how other people act or emote or how they think. So, that makes it extremely difficult to deal with those people around us. There are billions of people on this planet. That is billions of people who are all individuals who think and act and emote differently than you. And now we are all supposed to be thrown together and make it work somehow? That can be very challenging and can almost feel overwhelming and impossible at times.

No one person is the same, so you get different attitudes, different views, different behaviors, etc. This causes friction which then causes toxicity causing the trauma. But trauma can come from beautiful things as well, such as the loss of a loved one. When you have a beautiful connection with another person and then it abruptly ends. How do we deal with these traumatic events? Why do we go through them?

We need to ask ourselves what was meant to be learned from the experience? That does not mean that what happened to us was okay, and it may feel impossible to fathom that there was a positive lesson, but when you look at it closely, you will find it. Though extremely difficult, it is time to learn the positive lessons you were meant to learn, and through the positive lessons we can begin to heal ourselves. It is time to take your power back. Through deep reflection and meditation, you will find the answers.

Sending love and light!

INTUITIVE DISCOVERY

Today's lesson of the day is about exploring your intuitive side. Everyone in the world is born with natural intuitive gifts. Have you noticed you have very detailed dreams that suddenly come true? Do you feel things in your gut, as though you know something will happen, and it does? Do people who have transitioned to the spirit realm visit you in dreams? Do you feel other people's energies? No matter the intuitive gifts you have, it depends on whether you have chosen to explore them.

We have been told that our souls are in our bodies. But it is the other way around. We are just a small piece here on Earth. That means we always have one foot here, and one foot in the spirit realm. The great part about knowing this is to show you how powerful you really are. And this is a message from the spirit realm to start opening your mind to exploring the possibilities.

At a very young age we were taught that what we were seeing, hearing, or feeling was not real. And we learned to close the door on our gifts because, at that young age, we are extremely impressionable. It is time to reopen the door that has been shut for so long. But how does one do that? How can a person open themselves up like that after so many years? Is it even possible? And the answer is, yes!

It starts with raising your energy frequency. You need to surround yourself with positive energy. Positive people, environments, thoughts. This includes staying away from the news meant to keep us in fear. Then begin to explore meditation. Set an intention to connect to your higher-self. There is no right or wrong way to meditate as long as you have intention. Ask for answers. Ask to open the door again. Trust the process. It is time to remember who you truly are! Your journey starts now!

Sending love and light!!

ROMANTIC TRUST

Today's lesson of the day is to trust this new romantic journey that has begun. You have been hurt many times before. Through those negative experiences you have learned positive lessons: You will be respected. You will be treated as an equal. You will not be manipulated. You will support each other. You will create necessary boundaries.

In this new relationship you are taking your power back. You will no longer put someone else on a pedestal above you. You are the only person who has power over yourself. Do not give that power away. Just as your new partner should never give their power away. You are both strong and powerful individuals working together as a team to create something positive and beautiful. Joining your strong powers together. And this new beautiful relationship will last because that mutual respect is present and strong.

In the past, you tended to be with people because you were afraid to be alone. You needed someone in your life. However, needing someone gives your power away, and wanting someone takes your power back. But you have now learned this important lesson. You are no longer looking for someone to complete you because you are already complete. No part of you is missing.

That is why this new relationship that has begun is going to be different. Through learning these positive lessons, you will be able to have a very healthy, happy, and fulfilling relationship. You will finally know what it feels like to be in a relationship where anything and everything is possible because it is. Take your time, and enjoy this new and exciting journey. It could lead to something very beautiful. And this time you know you are deserving and enough. Always believe that, because that is the truth!

Sending love and light!!

OUR FURRY GUARDIANS

Today's lesson is about treating your pets with respect and kindness. Animals are magical beings. They have the abilities to bring us joy, make us laugh, protect us, and bring us comfort. They are extremely intuitive, and many times you will find that they know what you need before you know yourself. This can be from knowing when you are sick, when you are sad or depressed, when you need to be guarded, and even know when someone is pregnant.

The magic in animals is clear not only in our homes, but also in the wild. They keep the balance in the world and our ecosystems. We are all connected to each other because we are all one. We bring them into our homes, and we often feel healed by them when we need it most. They are our guardians and they know their jobs well. They are also energy healers. Your energy frequency raises positively when you are with them.

How about when they misbehave? Like human beings, animals have individual personalities of their own. What human being at any age does whatever they are supposed to a hundred percent of the time? None. How can we expect that of other beings that are here with us sharing this space? Just as your teenager is not always going to listen to you and sometimes rebels. Our pets are another being, not a mechanical robot.

You will notice that your pet chooses you and that you had them in your life when you needed them most. Their lives are so short, yet they show you unconditional love healing us from within. They are a very important member of your family. Make sure you treat them as the magical and special beings that they are. They have souls just as humans do. And one of the most important lessons they can teach us is unconditional love.

Sending love and light!!

SPIRITUAL PATIENCE

Today's lesson of the day is about being patient during your spiritual awakening. A spiritual awakening is not something that happens overnight. However, you are beginning to understand that there is more to this universe than what you know. People get so caught up on whose religion is correct when really none of that matters. Believe in something or nothing. That is your current journey.

We are simply on many different paths, and no path is alike. You have billions of journeys all happening at the exact same time on this planet, and all of those journeys intertwine and weave together like a beautiful dance. This is because we all come from the exact same place, which is all that is, everything everywhere all at once. Source. Call it whatever you would like. The name does not matter. We are all extensions of it. That means that we are all one with it.

As extensions of Source, the guides show a shirt that is woven. The shirt is Source. It is complete and whole. However, we all are one of the threads within the shirt. If you remove one of the threads from a shirt, the shirt is no longer whole. That means that each extension of Source is important not only on this planet, but every planet, dimension, and realm. Everything is a part of this woven fabric. Always know how important you are to the universe.

The road to your spiritual awakening will challenge you to open your mind to other ideas you have never known before. But it is all a part of the process as we continue to discover who we are. Meditation is important because it connects us to our higher-selves, and connecting to our higher-selves will get you closer to understanding. The answers will be revealed when it is time. Trust the process. You are closer to remembering who you truly are.

Sending love and light!!

NEGATIVITY AND GROWTH

Today's lesson is about understanding that we must go through negative experiences in our lives so that our souls can learn and grow. This is one of the toughest things to learn while we are here on Earth. In our natural state as souls, we do not get to experience negative events because the spirit realm is much too high of a frequency than it is here. This is where soul contracts come into play.

A soul contract is what you figuratively signed before returning to Earth school. It is a contract written up by not only you, but your spirit guides, light council, and soul group. The questions asked are: what do you want to learn this time around? Should you be wealthy or live a life of monetary struggle? Should you marry well or not? You decide which character to play, what occupation you will have, you decide the major challenges as well, and even how you will exit this plane of existence and when.

As souls, we need to know what it is like to go through every single type of event, emotion, hardship, love relationship, struggle, and so on. Without personally going through something and living it, whether positive or negative, your soul cannot learn fully, and grow. The more we grow, the closer we get to our own ascension. And that is the whole point of our soul's existence.

The image the guides show is a tornado. You hear about the devastation tornadoes bring from others or books or movies. However, you do not know fully until you have gone through it yourself. Same with our souls. We cannot understand something fully until we have gone through it. It is not always pleasant, but it is all a part of the design. There are no coincidences, and everything is happening for a reason. What positive lessons can we learn from these negative experiences? That is the important question.

Sending love and light!!

HEALING FROM THE PAST

Today's lesson of the day is about healing ourselves from past trauma so that we can live a much happier and fulfilling life. Negative events occur throughout our lives, and they can often affect us so much that they haunt us on a daily basis. These events can begin as early as birth. So, why do we need to face these traumatic events head on rather than shoving them deep down inside of us forever?

The aftermath of trauma does not just go away. If you shove something down deep within you, it will eventually come back up again. Something that is buried cannot be buried forever; at some point it will be unearthed. This affects how we have relationships, trying to figure out our life paths, and truly finding happiness and success for ourselves. Trauma is like a road block while driving. It brings everything to a halt, and life becomes even more challenging.

It is time to face your traumas because without facing them, you cannot heal from them. Facing trauma head on can feel extremely uncomfortable, and you may feel like giving up, but you are much stronger than you think. We are never given more than we can handle. It may feel like we are, but since everything is happening *for* us and not *to* us, you are much more resilient than you can imagine. Through facing trauma, we can finally begin to find peace.

Trauma in our lives causes a negative cloud that constantly hovers above us. And negativity will only attract more negativity which is why it is so difficult for people to move forward. It is time to get the help you need. There is no shame in asking for help. In fact, asking for help shows your strength. We must travel through the dense fog so that we can come out on the other side. It is time to begin this healing journey.

Sending love and light!!

BALANCE AND NEW RELATIONSHIPS

Today's lesson of the day is now that you have worked very hard at becoming emotionally balanced, you are ready for a new relationship. Before we can begin to love someone else fully, we need to love ourselves unconditionally. That is probably one of the most difficult things to do is love ourselves. We have grown up in a world that is obsessed with focusing on flaws.

We cannot control what the world thinks of us. We cannot control what others do or what they say. However, we can control what we think, say, and do for ourselves. You have done a remarkable job in shutting out the noise of the world. You look at yourself in the mirror and not only like what you see inside and out, but you love what you see. You are finally ready to meet someone who will treat you with the love and respect that you deserve.

There is someone you have had your eye on lately. They have the personality, the humor, and you are drawn to them. They are mutually attracted to you as well. They are attracted to the beautiful energy you give off and your newly found self-confidence. Through loving yourself, you have manifested this. Energies are attracted to those of the same energies. The more you love yourself and believe in yourself positively, the more you will attract someone of that same frequency.

Now is the time to get closer to the person and start getting to know them. There is a mutual attraction, so it is time to show them you are interested. It is time to take the leap and see where this new possibility can lead! You are taking control over your own power, and that is a beautiful thing! This is an exciting time, where you finally love yourself the way you were meant to and are ready to share it with someone else!

Sending love and light!!

THE EX

Today's lesson of the day is to find the calm while having to deal with an ex-spouse. You met someone and got married. You had a child or two which you both thought would help when marital issues arose, but instead, it just emphasized your problems. Things seemed to become so unbearable and cruel that the only solution to the problem was to get a divorce.

You really struggled with this because you put your children's needs first and you were willing to live in a life of complete misery rather than do what needed to be done about your marriage. However, you then realized that staying in the marriage was hurting your children because of all the intense fighting and name calling that was going on in front of them. So, the marriage ended, and then you were finally away from the person that had caused you so much pain and suffering and anxiety.

The most difficult part, is that you still must be a part of each other's lives until the children become adults. This means that even through trying to heal from the past trauma of the marriage, you are constantly reminded of it. You feel so betrayed. You saw a life for yourself when you were younger, and it was not like this at all. How are you supposed to move forward?

We need to remember that we cannot change other people. Since we cannot control others, we need to look inward. It is time to get ourselves to a place of calm because the anger and frustrations only make us angrier and more frustrated. We need to forgive the other person, not for them, but for ourselves, so we can start letting go of the negative energy. Then we need to forgive ourselves for allowing ourselves to be treated that way. Then our healing process can begin. Through meditation and therapy, you will move forward in your life.

Sending love and light!

SOUL SEARCHING

Today's lesson of the day is about doing some soul searching to remind ourselves how beautiful we all are. Life can be tough. It is meant to be a challenge, and that is an understatement. But today is about loving ourselves from the inside out, and trying to discover our true purpose. We are all beautiful beings sent here to remember who we are as souls. Everyone's soul-purpose is about helping others in some way.

This could mean helping others by making people laugh or feel entertained, teaching others, helping the sick feel better, giving to others less fortunate, helping people find their own life path, healing people's past traumas, etc. So many ways to be of service to humanity. If you are currently feeling lost and unsure of what you are meant to be doing, that is okay. We are not meant to discover the answers right away.

The first thing to do is stop worrying about your purpose. How can we discover and fully explore with mind fog giving us anxiety, fear, and doubt? Start by beginning to remove the fog. This can be through meditation, therapy, or both. The second thing to do is then ask yourself: What can I do to be of service to humanity that will bring me a lot of joy and fulfillment? Set that intention of self-discovery, and meditate on it.

Meditation will be an incredible addition to your self-care routine. In meditating, you are connecting to your higher-self and guides. Answers can come to you as visuals in your mind, through sound, and even smell. Take note of everything, but do not force it or have expectations. Close your eyes, set your intention, and just be. It may not happen immediately if meditation is new to you. However, you will eventually get the answers you are seeking.

Sending love and light!!

SELF-VALIDATION

Today's lesson of the day is about finding validation from within rather than from others. We all want to be told that we are doing a great job and get that pat on the back. There is a feeling of accomplishment when that happens. Others need validation due to low self-confidence within themselves, and if they do not receive the validation, they feel less than or unworthy.

This is when we need to start getting validation from ourselves. We are not always going to get that from others no matter how much we feel we need it at that time. Look back at the last five years, write a list of every single accomplishment. Do not be modest; really write down your accomplishments big and small. The size of the accomplishment does not matter because every accomplishment should be celebrated.

Look at your accomplishments in the last five years, and you will notice how long it is! You helped someone in need, paid it forward, got a promotion, healed from trauma, gave love to many people, discovered things about yourself, saved some money for something important, you were a true friend when it mattered, learned new skills, started practicing self-care, created something exciting, etc.

You do not need validation from others because you just validated yourself! That pride needs to come from within you. Because you are to be celebrated. You have had more victories than you think when you break it down and see them right in front of you! Now pat yourself on the back and take your amazing self out to dinner to celebrate! You are deserving, you are worthy, and you are enough!!!

Sending love and light!!

RESOLVING CONFLICTS

Today's lesson of the day is about resolving conflict with a person you are collaborating with. You have been working with this person for a while now, and your working relationship has started to sour. You are not in agreement with certain things, and it has become a real challenge and struggle. You were such good friends before, but things have shifted in a very negative direction which has caused a lot of tension and fighting.

This negativity is causing a toxic work environment, and you both refuse to see eye to eye. It is time to have an important conversation together at this time. Both of you need to be on the same page or this negative energy will continue to grow, and the negativity will continue to harm your relationship and business. You have worked so hard to get where you are, so you both need to decide if you are going to move forward together or separately.

What started this change? Was there a misunderstanding? Perhaps you have lost passion for the project. Maybe life at home has caused tension and anxiety that has affected one of your moods. When did the communication stop? Are you both able to turn this around so that you can be happy working together? What would happen to the project if one of you walked away?

These questions are not easy to answer, but they need to be asked. The fighting and toxicity need to end regardless because it is not doing either of you any good. Working together currently is doing more harm. What does your intuition tell you? Can you see this issue being resolved? It is time to have a meeting to have this conversation. And it must be done in a calm and respectful way. You worked as a team to start this project in the past, and you will need to work as a team to see if there is a future.

Sending love and light!!

PAST RELATIONSHIP REFLECTION

Today's lesson of the day is about taking time to reflect on past relationships before jumping into another one. As human beings we naturally enjoy companionship. However, you have had a string of many relationships that have not been very healthy, and the more negative experiences you have, the more negative you are feeling about yourself. It is time to take a long pause for some reflection.

As much as you want to be with someone, you need to understand what occurred in the last several relationships so you can understand the pattern. Maybe the people you have been attracted to do not treat you very well. Maybe they end up going back with their ex-partners. Maybe the people have been boring you and you feel like you are settling. It is time to put on the breaks.

This is when we need to look inward. Why are we meeting people like this? Why are they all so similar? The questions we need to answer are not about them but about ourselves. We are products of our environments. Maybe we grew up being people pleasers, we grew up with very low self-esteems, we were manipulated or abused in the past, etc. Patterns begin somewhere, and they often began before you sat down for your first date with a person.

It is time to put a hold on dating to self-reflect. Dig deep within yourself by journaling, therapy, or talking things out with others. As you discover the "whys," you will be able to understand what is going on. Understanding is learning. It is time to discover and explore your shadow-self. You will then notice a big difference in the people you meet on a romantic level because you looked inward first.

Sending love and light!!

TO MOVE FORWARD

Today's lesson of the day is about starting a new, major transition in life, and needing to contemplate how to move forward energetically. A massive chapter in your life has come to a close. You were not even sure if you were going to make it through, but you did, and you are ready for a new chapter to begin. You have a clean slate, so it is up to you to figure out how to move forward on this exciting new adventure.

Some chapters end with very painful events that leave us slightly paralyzed. It makes thinking of the future difficult because we fear for the worst. Again, you *can* control your experience here on Earth. If you feel everything around you will continue to fall apart, then the universe will provide. If you feel that everything around you *is* possible, the universe will provide. We are always manifesting even when we feel like we are not in control.

It is time to raise your energy frequency. Your thoughts, words, and actions matter. Every negative thought that you have is energy given to the universe. What you give out will come back to you energetically. How will you move forward into your new chapter? Your guides highly suggest going the more positive route for your journey. More doors will open to you, and life will not be as difficult or frustrating.

We must keep in mind that negative things will always happen around us, but we must decide how we will react. Always lead with compassion and love. A brand-new journey can be exhilarating and rewarding or terrifying and horrible. Continue in your meditation practices daily, and begin to visualize a beautiful future for yourself filled with positivity, love, happiness, and growth. You deserve the best life has to offer. Believe it and trust that there is a plan for you.

Sending love and light!!

SEEING THE BEAUTY

Today's lesson of the day is about seeing the beauty around you. It is easy to notice the negative things surrounding us in life. We often like to focus on what is wrong rather than focusing on what is right. The example the guides give is snow. As the snow falls, we immediately think of terrible traffic, angry drivers, accidents, horrible roads, shoveling, etc. The first sight of snow makes us furious, nervous, or anxious.

Our spirit guides talk about energy frequency a lot because it is literally everything. Furiousness, nervousness, and anxiousness are all low energy frequencies. And since we are all manifesting constantly, we need to be careful what we are manifesting. At the first sight of snow, if you picture in your mind that you will get in an accident, and you think about that image repeatedly, eventually, you will manifest an accident for yourself.

This is not the universe punishing you or judging you, it is simply giving you what you asked for. You have pictured this accident in your mind often and therefore it must be what you wish. The universe gifts you that experience. It is time to be extremely mindful of how you think and turn it around into a positive. What is beautiful about snow?

Look at its magnificence as it falls. Look how the ice crystals sparkle. What kind of fond memories does snow remind you of? Sledding as children, building a snowman, the smell in the air, snuggling by a warm, crackling fire? Perhaps snow is a symbol of slowing down for a moment in a fast-paced world. To take a moment to look around you and see the beauty. To take a pause. Suddenly, snow is no longer negative, but a positive symbol of stillness, togetherness, and joy. Try to do this with everything around you, and you will manifest beautiful things!

Sending love and light!!

WORKING AS A TEAM

Today's lesson of the day is about working as a team with your partner to start building a life together. You and your partner have been a couple for a while now, and all the signs are pointing towards creating the life you want for your futures. It is so important that you are growing together so that neither of you fall behind. If you have not discussed your future together yet, now is the perfect time to do that.

What are your dreams and desires? Do you both want to get married or not? Can you see yourselves building a home together? Do you both want children or not? Are you both stable monetarily? Have you always wanted pets? How have you both handled conflict together in the past? In what ways have you both stepped up to support each other? Do you both understand each other's love languages? How are you both with communicating with one another? Is there mutual respect? Are you both on the same page?

Sometimes these conversations can be difficult to talk about, but they are necessary. Meeting someone and falling in love with them is a beautiful thing, but what happens when life gets challenging? Communication is everything. As much as we want to believe life will always flow smoothly, it is not realistic. Through negative events that happen, will you grow together or apart? Are you willing to commit even through the hard times?

As our soul grows the most during negative experiences, so do our relationships if they are strong enough. It is remembering that you are both a team. And when you are a team, anything and everything is possible. An equal partnership. This is a new chapter and a new journey in your book. You owe it to yourselves to make it a beautiful one if that is what you wish!!

Sending love and light!!

HEALING FROM LOSS

Today's lesson of the day is healing from past loss so that you can start your new beautiful journey. When we go through a lot of emotional pain and grief, we find it almost impossible to move forward. A large cloud or fog seems to stop us in our tracks. On the outside people think you are incredibly strong, but deep inside you are falling apart. You will not be able to move forward until you face the pain that you have hidden from within.

Sometimes it is the fear of forgetting what we have been through. The guilt of moving on. There is always a grieving process. Grieving people we have lost, grieving a life we were supposed to have, grieving our childhood. But at some point, a healing must begin. If you do not begin to heal, your mind starts replaying things over again like a broken record.

This means that you begin the grieving process all over in a continuous loop, and you cannot get out of it. However, it is time to end the cycle. It is affecting your family, your career, your connections around you, and you feel as though you do not have a purpose in life anymore. This is because you cannot see through the thick fog in front of you, and you feel lost.

But know that you are not as lost as you may think. You know deep down it is time to start the process of moving forward, and it is a decision only you can make. Therapy and grief counseling are perfect ways to begin this new healing journey. And once you face everything, you will notice the fog start to slowly lift, and you will see the world of possibility again. You will finally see the clear path in front of you, and you can begin the new chapter of your incredible journey! Trust the process.

Sending love and light!!

PASSION IN THE DRIVER'S SEAT

Today's lesson of the day is about taking a passion that you have and turning it into a successful career. You have been working a regular job for a while now. You have noticed that you are going through the motions, and you almost feel like a robot most days. You get up, go to work, come home, eat, go to bed, and do the same thing again the next day and the next.

However, deep inside of you is this yearning for something more. You have even written it down in a journal or have told a close friend or family member. There is something you are very passionate about that you would love to pursue, but there is some fear and doubt involved. Your intuition is trying to show you your path, but your ego pops in giving you the fears and doubts.

The truth is we are not meant to help realize *other* people's dreams, we are here to realize our own. What about what you want in life? Every person on this planet has a soul purpose. Something we were meant to do while here. Usually this involves serving humanity in some way that makes you excited and passionate. You already know what it is because it burns from within you and calls to you on a regular basis.

The moment has come to take the leap and start to make this passion of yours come to life. It is the time to push all your fears and doubts aside and trust this yearning desire for more in life. You are capable of anything. You will be creating something that you will be proud of and making a difference in the world. It is time to stop being the robot committed to realizing other people's dreams. It is now time for you to begin realizing your own.

Sending love and light!!

BATTLE SCARS

Today's lesson of the day is that our scars on our bodies tell a story, and to be proud of the battle scars you have. Throughout our lives we go through some big events positive or negative that leave us with some visible scarring. Something positive like a child being born or something negative like a very difficult surgery from our past. It is natural to want to hide these scars from the world because we are taught at an early age from the media and magazines that beauty is on the outside.

We immediately try to think of ways we will have to hide them. Buying new clothes to pretend they do not exist. Even though perfection is only created with an airbrush, we still feel we need to look a certain way to be accepted into society. But the one thing we forget is the actual purpose for the scar in the first place.

Maybe this is your first child or even your third, and your scar shows the building of your beautiful family over time. Maybe you got into a fight when you were younger that left you with a scar as you tried to defend yourself. Maybe it was from an accident that tells you to be more careful and mindful in the future. Maybe you had cancer that you had battled, and the scar is a reminder that you are a fighter.

Whatever the reason for the scar(s) on your body, they tell the story of our lives. We are each a book on the shelf of the universe, and we all have our own unique and individual stories. We should be proud of those scars and show them off. Show people your strength and resilience. Because as we continue our journeys, our battle scars show that we do not give up, and that we are true warriors. No more hiding or being embarrassed by them. Be proud of your strength and how far you have come!

Sending love and light!!

GETTING THAT PROMOTION

Today's lesson of the day is to celebrate because you will be getting a promotion soon!! Good things come to those who wait, and you have been waiting a while now to get this promotion at work; the next step in your career. You have the knowledge, the experience, the work ethic, and the positive energy necessary to move forward. However, sometimes you doubt yourself if you are even good enough or capable of doing the job. It is time to push the ego aside.

The ego is helpful for a few reasons. For instance, the ego puts the fear into us when we are about to get into an accident, and forces us to react quickly. Another example is if you are walking alone at night down a dark street and you realize that it is probably not a good idea to go any further so you take a taxi home. When we are in possible danger.

The feelings of fear and doubt you are currently having about this promotion are an unnecessary reaction. The ego is not needed at this moment. It is time to shove the ego away by filling yourself with positive energy. And how can we do that? We celebrate ourselves with every accomplishment big or small. When you get that promotion you have been hoping for, know that you are deserving of it.

Once you get the promotion, take yourself out to dinner, bring your family and friends to join you. Put that beautiful energy of celebration and love into the universe so that you can continue to manifest wonderful things in your life. You are deserving, you are worthy, you are enough. Everything in life happens for a reason, so it is time to let go and trust the process. Congratulations on your future journey! It is going to be a great one!

Sending love and light!!

WORK AND HOME TUG OF WAR

Today's lesson is about the importance of a work and home balance. Sometimes we find ourselves so busy at work that we feel we need to shove our personal lives aside. Balance is so important in every aspect of our lives. If you are constantly bringing work home, even if you have left the office, you have literally brought the office to you. So, you are still at work regardless of your surroundings.

At what point is enough, enough? At what point do you say, "this can wait for tomorrow?" What happened to your own personal needs? How are you supposed to unwind and focus on yourself and your family? Bringing work home also creates a disconnect between you and your family that can affect your relationships in the future. It is time to create those necessary, healthy boundaries.

Boundaries are so important. Without them, we are taken advantage of. It is very easy for people to demand our precious time, and the reaction we have is often one of worry. "If I do not work fifteen hours a day, the company will no longer see my value, and they will get rid of me." Oftentimes, we just feel like a number at a massive corporation who have very little interest in our wellbeing.

This is the moment to evaluate how you balance your time. Make sure to set a time for dinner so that you are present with your family every day. Put away the phones and distractions so you can focus on the important people around you. And when you get home, no more work. Once you set boundaries, you will feel much more at ease rather than having your time monopolized, leaving you more stressed, worried, and unable to sleep. Your health and happiness are important too. Never forget that.

Sending love and light!!

LOST OPPORTUNITY

Today's lesson of the day is about understanding why you lost an opportunity you have been hoping for. The big rule to remember is that everything is happening *for* us not *to* us. It is very easy to immediately go into a victim mentality where we scream out, "why are you doing this to me?!" to Source or our spirit guides. However, it is time to consider the reasons the opportunity was taken away in the first place.

Our guides and Source have nothing but our best interest at heart, they could be protecting you from something. What could they be protecting you from? It was an opportunity you had your heart set on! There are no mistakes in this universe. Even though we have some free will, like ad-libbing during a play, we still end up sticking to the script that was written before the play began.

Your guides are there to make sure you stay on track. They are your stage managers during your performance. So, why the lost opportunity? For a few reasons: because the opportunity that you really wanted here on Earth was not meant to be a part of your experience, it could have possibly gotten you too far off track from your soul's goals, your spirit guides needed to protect you from something, or there is a better opportunity coming up for you.

If something does not go the way you wanted it to, consider one of those reasons above. There are no mistakes, no accidents, and everything happens for a reason. When you stop for a moment, contemplate, and give into divine intervention, you realize your guides are there to help and assist you. Know that everything takes time, and you are always headed in the right direction. Trust the process. Everything will make sense as your "life's play" unravels.

Sending love and light!!

YOUR BEST INTEREST

Today's lesson of the day is to trust your intuition when you feel someone close to you does not have your best interest at heart. We cannot control other people on this planet; we can only control ourselves. But there will be times when someone close to you may try to manipulate you to get what they want. Just because someone is a friend or a family member, it does not obligate you to do everything they say. It is time to listen to your intuition.

Perhaps someone is constantly demanding something from you to prove you are a good family member or a good friend. The question that should be asked is why do you need to prove anything at all? You are worthy of love regardless. You have been manipulated in the past, and there is a pattern. Sometimes we like to ignore those signs because we do not want to think negatively about our loved ones. But when will you decide to take your power back?

We are individuals first and foremost. We are taught at an early age to give our power to others, and if you do not, then you are not a loyal person. So, we end up giving our power away to people over the years as we grow into adulthood and beyond. It is at this point that we begin to lose our identity. How can we be individuals if we are living for others needs and not our own?

Take your power back. You have placed other people on a pedestal above you. This does not mean to disrespect them, this means that you will not allow yourself to be taken advantage of. All relationships, whether it is family, friends, work relationships, etc., are a two-way street. It is all about the balance of give and take. If you are constantly giving and giving and you are never receiving, you will find yourself depleted of your precious energy. Begin to find the balance in your relationships, and you will be so relieved that you did!

Sending love and light!!

SLEEP IS HEALING

Today's lesson of the day is making sure you are getting enough sleep so that your body can heal itself naturally. You are the type of person who does not sleep very much, and you may only get a few hours of sleep a night. But while we are sleeping is when our body heals itself, so sleep is more important than ever. Our souls do not need sleep; our soul can go on forever without resting or meditating or sleeping. These things are only important to maintain our physical bodies.

Just like it is important that we are careful what we put into our bodies, such as what we eat and drink, it is time to be more mindful of what your body needs to keep it working at an optimum level; because our bodies are extremely precious. Working out during the week is also included in keeping our vessels strong.

While here on Earth we experience viruses and bacterial infections, and by sleeping, your immune system strengthens. When you work out by lifting weights, sleep helps to repair the muscles making them stronger. Sleep also helps with mental health by improving your mood, and reducing stress and anxiety among many other things. The question is how much sleep is not enough or too much?

The amount is different for everyone. The key is waking up refreshed and feeling good. If you wake up groggy, dragging your body, you did not get enough sleep. If you slept for twelve hours and you have those same symptoms, you got too much. Only you know that sweet spot where you feel at your best. So, aim for that amount of sleep every night, so that you can feel the difference. Our bodies are fascinating vehicles, but like a car, they need to be well taken care of.

Sending love and light!!

SOCIAL MEDIA HORRORS

Today's lesson of the day is about the fears and anxieties that come from social media and how it affects us energetically. In the days before social media, we were not surrounded by world events or politics or other negative issues every single moment of every single day. Information was not so easily or readily available. But why is this a negative thing? Isn't it good to be informed?

The answer is yes; it is good to be informed. But there is a difference between being informed and becoming obsessive. Every day, most people spend a significant amount of time on their phones, and they are not only informed, they are obsessed by the drama, the fights, the threats, the aggression, the adrenaline rush. Negative energy can be addictive, and it is easy to get caught up in the middle of it. And once you are hooked, just like any other addiction, it is very hard to control or stop.

Why is negative energy addicting? Why do we love drama? Because it excites us. The ego is a powerful thing, but it is only a human trait, and has nothing to do with our soul itself. Ego comes from the human mind where addiction and fear and anger come from. Why do we like scary movies? Because it gives us a rush. Why do we watch the news when we know it will make us angry? Because deep down we love the drama, we get to fight with others with no consequence.

However, it is time to be careful how much you are around these negative energy frequencies. Every negative thought, negative word you say, and every negative action you take has energy connected to it. This energy flows through the universe, and the universe will give you the same energy in return. It is time for you to take control and know when to walk away. You will notice a positive shift in your life so that amazing things can happen to you.

Sending love and light!!

HEALING FROM THE BACKSTABBER

Today's lesson of the day is someone has stabbed you in the back, and now it is time to begin to heal. You are a very trusting person, and that is a beautiful trait. Never lose your ability to trust. However, some people in this life will take advantage of your trust and kindness. They see you as an easy target to prey on. You did nothing to deserve this kind of treatment. Luckily, you are away from this person and you can start to reflect.

Through reflection you can begin to heal and understand. We need to consider why this person in your life created this drama to begin with. Most of the time it is a confidence issue. They do not feel like they are enough. Or it could be narcissism. Those are just a couple examples out of the many possibilities. There is always a reason why someone behaves the way they do.

Now you need to look within yourself. Why were you the perfect target? It could be your beautiful positive energy you emit. It could be your beautiful confidence and personality. It could be the opportunities you have been given. It could be your strength and determination. It could be that you are easily loved by others without even trying. It could be all of the above. You are a target because you are full of the light that they wish they had themselves.

A leach unapologetically removes your life force from your body, just as a toxic person tries to dim and steal your light. You have decided to cut ties with them for your own good. However, do not keep these feelings bottled up within you. It will be important to get these emotions and negative energy out of your body. Through this healing, make sure to keep those beautiful qualities you have. Do not lose them because they are a precious and powerful gift.

Sending love and light!!

ANOTHER POINT OF VIEW

Today's lesson of the day is when fighting with another person, try to understand the fight from the other person's point of view. When we have an argument with someone else, it is very easy to see things only from our side. But there are always two sides to every story, and it is important to be open and see the full picture.

Why is someone fighting with you? Why did they lash out? Regardless of why one of you began this argument in the first place, there is always a deeper reason. One of you may be having a very difficult time at home or work. Perhaps one of you are unhappy in your love life? Maybe there is a struggle with other family members. Is one of you being constantly bullied by others outside of this situation and this was the straw that broke the camel's back? Is there a substance abuse issue that causes one of you to be on edge constantly?

There is a reason for ours and others' actions. No one wakes up one morning planning to have their own day ruined by starting a fight. Regardless if the person you are struggling with seems to enjoy starting drama, there is always a reason. Perhaps they do not have control over their own lives at home, and therefore feel the desperate need to control other situations in unhealthy ways elsewhere.

It is time to look at this situation from another point of view. It does not make the situation okay, but trying to understand where the other person is coming from helps to gain some perspective. Maybe understanding this will help you to let go of the negative energy for the good of yourself. We cannot control others, only ourselves, so perhaps it is time for you to end the fight since this is hurting you energetically. It is time to be the bigger person so that you can move forward in a healthier way.

Sending love and light!

WE ARE ALL CONNECTED

Today's lesson of the day is that we are all connected to each other's stories. Our actions matter not only with friends, family, and acquaintances, but also with those we have never met. People you are driving with on the road, people at the grocery store, etc. We have a choice in how we treat others because whether you know it or not, we affect other people's lives.

For example, you are driving down the road and someone is going slow in front of you. But once you can get around them, you drive up, scream some obscenities, maybe a rude hand gesture, then speed off. You have no idea what kind of day that person was having. You do not know why the person was driving so slowly. Regardless of the reason, you have now affected that person's day further. Since energy ripples outward, it not only affects the person you screamed at, but now it will affect those who are around that person for the remainder of the day.

Just as negative energy spreads, so does positive energy. Perhaps someone calls you from an insurance company, and they have spoken to twenty people who have just yelled at them for the last three hours. An act of kindness and understanding from you can change someone's day. Or you see a homeless person on the street and you give them money if you are able. Your act of kindness may have just changed their life.

It is time to consider the impact you have on others around you. If you find yourself getting frustrated, take a moment and take three very deep breaths. It will release the negative energy that you have building up inside. Remember negative energy does not last forever. Think of it like a cloud you can walk through. Instead, consider positive energy when interacting with others. You have the power to brighten up someone's day, and that ripple effect is a beautiful one!

Sending love and light!!

THE VICIOUS CYCLE

Today's lesson of the day is about making the important decision to start healing from a traumatic loss in your life. You have felt trapped in this vicious cycle of grief, anger, and sadness, and you seem to be going in a loop day after day after day. As time passes, you are reliving this painful event as though it happened yesterday, but it has been some time now, and your mind continues to flood constantly.

You fear that if you stop grieving or stop reliving the painful memories, that you will start to forget or you are afraid that ending the grief will somehow dim the light on how significant the event was. This simply is not true. Trauma is different than a memory. Traumatic events give you not only mental and emotional symptoms, but physical symptoms as well. A memory is the ability to recall information, and this recollection has no effect on you the way trauma does.

It is time for you to decide whether to begin the healing process or continue this torturous cycle. One thing is for sure; you do not deserve this kind of torture day in and day out. So, it is very important to choose the path of healing. If you do not already have a therapist, it will be very important to have one; one that does EMDR (Eye Movement Desensitization and Reprocessing) treatment. EMDR takes the traumatic files from one side of the brain and shifts them to regular memories that you can process in a healthier way.

It is time to take back control of your life because you have given up your power for so long. It is time to begin to heal. The negative energy attached to you is only doing you harm. Remember to give yourself love, compassion, and grace through this process. Healing is not an easy journey, but you are a warrior that is capable of incredible things! Trust the process.

Sending love and light!!

PASSION DISCOVERY

Today's lesson of the day is about discovering your passion and making it happen. Many times, we overthink things. We are not sure if life is as simple as following your bliss, but it is. But know that our bliss can change throughout our lives. What you may be passionate about at one point in your life, you might suddenly be blissful about something else in another. Life paths are not straight ahead; there are many twists and turns.

When you were younger, you always wanted your life to go a certain way, and then you made it happen. But now, years later, you are realizing that that part of you is no longer excited. You are now just going through the motions. This can also be confusing and frustrating how something that made you so happy and fulfilled in the past no longer fills your cup.

It is time to think of things in a different way. Remember that everything happens for a reason. You are exactly where you are meant to be at this time. You needed to learn a certain skill so that you could prepare yourself for your next chapter and adventure. It was not a waste of time. You were gaining new skills and knowledge that will aid you in the next part of your life journey.

We are not meant to do the same thing day in and day out for the rest of our lives. When we feel it is time to move on to a new passion, it is important for us to listen to our inner calling. Life is meant to be exciting, not monotonous. It is time to discover what you are passionate about in this new phase of your life! How can the skills and knowledge you have acquired help you? Do not let fear get in the way. Push the ego aside and follow your intuition. When you do that, fulfillment is just around the corner.

Sending love and light!!

INTUITIVE SURRENDER

Today's lesson of the day is about listening to your intuition. You have a new great idea! This could be something to do with your new passion in life, it could be starting a business, it could be a new hobby, etc. Whatever this new big idea is, it is a great one, and you know deep down that it is the answer to all the questions you have been asking yourself. But this new idea popped into your head for a reason. It was placed there by either your higher self or your guides to act upon.

This new idea in your mind seems to come in and out repeatedly in your head. Your higher-self or guides are not letting you forget about it. You know that you need to act on this new idea, but you are suddenly hearing voices of self-doubt and fear: Are you sure you can handle that? If you take this risk, it is not going to work out. Maybe you are not ready yet.

The ego is a powerful thing. It tells us when we are in horrible danger, and tries to protect us from doing harm to ourselves. This is a fantastic thing when it comes to our immediate safety. However, our egos can also be harmful to us because of giving us those fears and worries and doubts when it is unnecessary. We need to learn to push our egos aside. If you need an answer to something, close your eyes and connect with your higher-self.

Ask yourself if this is a good idea. Your intuition will always be the first answer you hear. It is always working a hundred percent of the time. It is a quick moment after that your ego pops in with doubt and fear. Always trust your intuition, you will feel it in your gut. If you feel excitement and a lightness, do it! If you feel a heaviness or your stomach is dropping, do not. Trust in your higher-self because your higher-self is always there to support you; it is you.

Sending love and light!!

GOD IS NOT A WEAPON

Today's lesson of the day is that some will use God (Source) as a weapon against others. For thousands of years, people have used God as a reason to force others into submission in the name of power, greed, manipulation, and control; the opposite of what Source is. Whatever you want to call it: God, Source, etc., it is nothing but unconditional love.

It does not matter what religion, sexual orientation, gender, race, nationality, etc. that you are. It also does not matter if you do not believe in anything at all. None of it matters or has any bearing whatsoever on whether God loves you. We are all a part of it, an extension. This is simply the life you wanted to experience this go around. How did we get so "lucky" to incarnate here? The answer is simple. It was our choice; and Earth is one of the most challenging places anywhere to incarnate.

Our souls grow the most through extremely difficult experiences. The more negative the event, the more we learn and grow from it. The negatively charged people around us are put here to test us, attempt to drag us down to their frequency so that we can reach ultimate growth by resisting. Remember, our soul's main goal is to "level up" so much that it never has to return. That is a hefty task, but that is the journey we are all on.

Negative energy frequencies are anger, fear, frustration, manipulation, doubt, sadness, etc. It is so important that we keep our energy frequencies as high as possible: love, joy, peace, laughter, creativity, and hope. If you do not like the world you are in, be the change you want to see in the world. If you meet people with anger, anger will be reflected back to you. Some may use God as a weapon against you, but deep down you know the truth: God is unconditional love.

Sending love and light!!

STANDING UP FOR PEOPLE

Today's lesson of the day is to stand up for your loved ones. Sometimes people we love have a hard time standing up for themselves or need some extra support. It is so important that we are all there for each other in a positive way. Life is about community. Without community there is not a whole lot that we can do on our own. It takes working together and team work.

Whether you can see it now or not, the world is slowly changing to a higher energy frequency with a major focus on togetherness. People looking out for each other. This is due to the positive energy frequency of the collective rising every day. The spiritual awakening as a collective is inevitable, and you will have those who will understand, and those who will try to fight it without success.

My guides show there is going to be much less government with much more focus on community. There will be a major realization that we are all one, and helping others in our communities is also helping ourselves. Anything that is of a low energy vibration will no longer have any importance in our lives because it will not serve us. This means we should try to start living in this new beautiful energy today.

It is important to be there for your loved ones. Care about your neighbors, your family, and friends. Have balanced relationships of give and take with all people you meet. Make sure you all have a cup that is being filled. Stay in a positive energy frequency as much as possible. Positive energy is beautiful and infectious, and those who are around you will feel it and reflect it back to you and others. The spiritual shift of the world is coming, and it will be glorious!

Sending love and light!!

SAFE DRIVING

Today's lesson of the day is about driving safety. You may feel like this lesson is a little odd, but it is not. Our guides are here to guide and protect us whenever possible. And since we have free will, our safety matters in all cases. So, driving safety it is! There are a few things they would like to address here:

The first is about driving recklessly. Make sure to maintain a safe speed. You will see people driving extremely fast and weaving in and out of cars like it is a game. They are playing a dangerous game of chance. As nerve wracking as that is, do not forget that they are being taught lessons too, so maintain your distance from them. Just as others cannot control your actions, you cannot control other's actions, and that could cause an accident. Rules are put in place for safety. Rules are not suggestions.

Patience is not an easy thing to learn while you are driving. You sit behind people who are driving slowly and it starts to make you crazy. Your ego starts popping in and tells you to get frustrated and act out. But you do not know why they are driving so slowly, and it really does not matter. It is time to learn patience. Instead, take three very deep breaths and imagine a ball of negative energy flowing out of your body through your exhale. You will soon continue on your way.

Do not drive while on substances, certain medications, or with a fever. There are always options to get to your destination without endangering your life and others. If you are not feeling well, and no one can drive you, call emergency services, or a driving company. This also includes drinking before driving. Take time to sober up before getting into a car or take other means of transportation. Drive safely!

Sending love and light!!

TAKE YOUR TIME WITH NEW CONNECTIONS

Today's lesson of the day is to take your time with this new connection you have made recently. You just met someone new, and you have started dating them. You have never met someone so incredible who clicks with you the way they do. Your mind starts racing about all the future possibilities. That is a beautiful thing to have found this brand-new connection, but this is a reminder that it is time to take things slow. You are not living in the present.

What happens when we rush the process? You are living in the future. By not living in the now, you are missing out on truly getting to know the person. By not living in the present, you are not really connecting to them, and this can cause issues within the relationship. If you are always thinking five steps ahead, the person you have connected with may become distant.

You could also miss some important red flags when you move too quickly. Everyone that we meet shows their true self bit by bit as we get to know them and they get more comfortable. No one can truly hide who they are for a long-extended period. So, as you get to know someone, their true self emerges, and you will see if they are someone you truly want in your life. This takes time.

Lastly, enjoy the journey. This is a new adventure. Patience is taking the time to love and savor every minute. Take your past knowledge from relationships you have had and learn from them. That knowledge is power. Just like any adventure there will be twists and turns, and with the knowledge you have gained, you will be able to navigate through better than before.

Sending love and light!!

WEAPONIZING RELIGION

Today's lesson of the day is that believing in any or all or no religion leads you to the same place; do not use religion as a weapon. We are all here to have an individual experience of our choosing amongst many other souls doing the same. We are all connected. We are all one, just in different forms. In the end we are all choosing to have this exact experience, at this exact moment, in this exact body, learning these exact lessons. Now back to religion.

Religions were created from ideas that certain ascended masters such as Buddha, Jesus, Yogananda, Babaji, among many others, had. These ascended masters had a deep connection with the spirit realm, being able to step in and out easily to access information. They mastered intuitive techniques that allowed them to learn this information. Through their findings, they took that information and shared it with people which of course shook things up around them.

You will notice when you take the positive teachings from every religion, many aspects are similar: leading with love and compassion, kindness, respect, inclusion, and peace. Human beings in positions of power are the ones who wanted control over others by creating all the negative aspects of each religion: violence, extremism, hate, exclusion, and fear. These ascended masters' teachings have been misused for thousands of years.

The guides show the image of your hand. Every finger leads to the same place, the palm. Therefore, no religion is better than another. In regard to Hell, the scary place of damnation, it does not exist. Hell was created to control others by keeping them in fear and keep them in line. Regardless of what you believe or if you do not believe in anything at all, we are all returning to the same place together: Home.

Sending love and light!!

BELIEVING IN YOURSELF

Today's lesson of the day is taking action to make your dreams come true and believing in yourself. You have explored so many options in the past, and now you have come up with an idea that will bring you joy and fulfillment; your soul's purpose. Today is the day to start putting your dreams and goals into action. The first step to doing that is believing in yourself and knowing that you are more than capable and worthy. Today is the day to put fears and doubts aside.

Not all our ideas are our own. Many ideas and thoughts are put into our minds by our spirit guides, angels, and even our ancestors who have transitioned. They are all there to help us stay on track with our soul's mission, but it is our job to listen and allow ourselves to be guided. They are extremely creative how they get messages to us.

Whenever you have an "aha!" moment, ask yourself why that just happened. There are constant signs all around us: whenever an idea pops into your mind that excites you, you overhear something that gives you a thought, or a song comes on the radio confirming everything; it is time to listen and take note. If you ask someone a question and they give you an incredibly wise response, perhaps you should consider listening rather than ignoring it.

Now it is time for the next big step which is gathering the courage and strength to take the risk. You do not have much fulfillment lately because you are not being driven by passion. This means you are not on the right path. Our life paths are ones that light something within us. Every person on this planet has a soul purpose, but many times people are too afraid of taking the leap. Your soul's purpose is calling to you loud and clear, and your journey starts today!!

Sending love and light!!

TRAPPED

Today's lesson of the day is if you are trapped in an abusive relationship, it is time to get out of it. When we are finding love in our lives, there are certain people who are very good at hiding their true selves. Perhaps you have seen snippets of it over time when they were under the influence or without. There are always red flags at the beginning, but sometimes the red flags seemed small or insignificant at the time.

Time has passed, however, and you know that this person you are with is not who you signed up for. They are cruel, have violent outbursts, say horrible things, and gaslight you. But there is a problem; you have married them and you may have children with them. Suddenly, you feel stuck; you feel there is no way you would be able to get out of it now. But you know that you deserve way better than you are getting, and you certainly do not deserve this treatment; no one does. It is time to make the decision to leave.

Your abusive partner has slowly cut your ties from the outside world and isolated you. You do not have a job or money of your own. How can you even consider leaving especially when you have children? Remember that there are always options. Call a friend or a family member. Call the domestic abuse hotline. Create a plan. Remember that even though you feel bound and imprisoned by this toxic person, you have the power to release yourself. It is time to gather your strength.

The first step is recognizing that the environment you are living in is not healthy for you or for your children. You are not alone even when you feel you are. It is time to take your power back because the person you are with had no business taking your power to begin with. You had to go through this experience for a reason, but enough is enough and it is time to act! You are a warrior!! Believe it!!

Sending love and light!!

THE MENTAL HEALTH
JOURNEY

Today's lesson of the day is it is time to begin your new mental health journey. Whether you have depression or anxiety, among other conditions, they can be extremely crippling. Depression and anxiety are low frequencies, and it is never your fault if you are going through this; however, it is also no coincidence that other negative things have been happening around you at the same time.

The universe does not discriminate. It does not matter what you are going through because everything is based on energy. So, if you have tons of anxiety and depression, the law of attraction goes into effect. The energy you put out will come back to you in return. It is easier said than done, but it is time to raise your energy frequency so that the universe gives you more positive energy in return.

There are many ways to raise our frequencies. One is meditation. Meditation everyday gets you to a place of calm and helps lower stress and anxiety, and depression. Guided meditations online are easily accessible. Another important option is be careful what you watch and listen to. This includes what you see on social media and the news. Watch and listen to programs that make you laugh, make you feel good, and make you feel comforted. Stay away from all programs that make you angry, anxious, scare you, or make you even more depressed. It will only make things worse.

Nothing is hopeless or impossible. Realize that it is time to act and try these tools to raise your frequency. If you need extra support, therapy is an incredible resource to aid you in your journey. Now you have incredibly effective tools in your toolbox. Nothing is ever impossible.

Sending love and light!!

WE ARE NOT OUR PAST

Today's lesson of the day is that we are not our past; if you have not been good to others, you are able to make the conscious decision to change. It is time to reflect on your past now. We are human, and we make mistakes. We have all done things that we regret. Maybe you were cruel to someone else. Maybe you stole something from someone in the past. Maybe you enjoyed getting into fights. Perhaps you created drama for others.

As much as we would all like to believe that we are all saints, we are not perfect. Not only have we made mistakes in our past, but we will continue to make them. Life here is not easy, but we can learn from how we have behaved in the past so that we can make our present a bit brighter and grow from that knowledge. It is time to reflect on how you have treated other people before today. How did you affect other people's lives in a negative way?

272

This is a difficult question to answer because we do not want to see ourselves in the negative, but we are able to change once we evaluate our behavior. Looking at your past self, what would you do differently? Why did you behave the way you did? There is always a deeper reason why we act the way we do.

Now, once you sit with those questions for a bit, perhaps it is time to answer those questions honestly, and then figure out what positive lessons you could learn from your past behaviors. Do not judge yourself, learn from yourself. Since we are always changing and shifting, how do you want the new you to be? How does the you of today treat others? How does the new you deal with issues occurring in your life without taking it out on others? We are not our pasts, so it is now time for you to make a choice and make a positive change for the now.

Sending love and light!!

MANIFESTING SUCCESS

Today's lesson of the day is about manifesting your success and relationships. Many times, we wish for what we want to happen in our lives. We say things such as "I would like to have –" or "I wish I could find –" When saying things like this, you are saying you hope to have it sometime in the future. Since time is only linear on this planet, the universe does not recognize when you should receive what you are asking for. So, how do we manifest for what we want in the now?

The beautiful thing about being human beings, is that we are wonderful manifestors. Human beings do this naturally. We need to also be aware that not only can we manifest positive things in our lives but also negative things as well. For example: if you envision yourself getting pulled over by the police and getting a ticket, and you see this happening in your mind often enough, it will happen.

Manifesting for ourselves is as simple as having the thought itself. The only difference is that you do not ask or wish for the universe to give you what you are wanting. You manifest by telling the universe you already have it. "I have an amazing partner. I have the career I have always wanted. I have a house with an attached garage, a finished basement, etc."

Envision whatever it is you want as though you already have it. The universe will know it to be so and make it happen much faster than if you would have wished it to be sometime in the future. Now, go get what you want in life, after all, you already have it! It is true if you say it is true! Happy manifesting!

Sending love and light!!

WALLS YOU HAVE BUILT

Today's lesson of the day is that it is time to decide to tear down the walls you have put up throughout your life. You had put up walls gradually since you were younger to protect yourself from emotional distress. But you are realizing now that those walls that were meant to protect you originally are now harming you later in life.

You are finding that these walls have affected your romantic relationships, your relationships with family, your ability to make friends, keep a job, or trust others. Remember that life is a bunch of choices to create your experience. You made a choice to put the walls up, but now it is time to make the choice to tear the walls down. Those walls were not built on solid ground or in a healthy manner to begin with.

It is time to build on more solid ground. To start with a sturdier foundation. The only way this can happen is starting fresh. This can be done with therapy, meditation, or all the above to get you to that place. These unsteady walls are currently not serving you, so you have a big decision to make.

In your mind, see the way you want your life to be at this moment. Visualize it. Manifest it. Remember that anything and everything is possible, but the healing must start from deep within first. Once you face it head on, you will be unstoppable!

Sending love and light!!

FEAR OF HAVING IT ALL

Today's lesson of the day is about facing your fears of losing everything you have now that you have gotten it. Everything is going amazing for you right now. You have manifested incredible things for yourself: relationships, career, love, a home, family, security. And now that you have gotten what you have desired, you are constantly afraid that everything will be taken away from you.

Contrary to what others may say, getting everything can be scary and nerve racking because if life is meant to be a mixture of positive and negative experiences, it is only a matter of time before the wind changes, correct? However, it is so important not to think this way because you may begin manifesting negative things in your life.

It is so important to live in the present moment. Living in the future is only going to make you feel unsettled all the time. If you live in the present and focus on the joys and the love you are currently feeling, you will have a much more positive time as you continue through this simulated adventure called the human experience.

It is natural, with our human ego minds, that we live and worry for tomorrow, but how would things change for the better if we lived for today? For this moment? See the positive things that are happening around you right now. Feel them, enjoy them, take them all in. Savor every moment of joy because it is meant to be savored. Life is happening for you, not to you, so it is time to stop fearing what could be, and enjoy what is – today. Stop and smell the beautiful roses, they will certainly make you smile!

Sending love and light!!

COLLABORATION

Today's lesson of the day is that when starting a new business you are wanting to start, sometimes it is best to collaborate with a partner. You have been wanting to start a business, but you may not be as business savvy as you would like to think you are. Perhaps it is time to bring in someone who understands the business side of things to help your creative idea come to life. Two heads are sometimes better than one, and it will certainly give you peace of mind that everything will be done correctly.

Who would you be able to find to join you on this new adventure? Well, it should be someone who shares your vision for this new business. We are all here to serve each other in the best way we can, so having that same vision is important. Remember when you are starting this new business that it needs to be about what you are trying to do for others than just the money.

It is true that we need money to survive in this current reality, but when that is what is driving you to open this business, you will never feel fulfilled within it; that is because your purpose would be self-serving. Make sure your passion to open this business is the driving force to help others in whatever way excites you both. Once you have the passion and the drive, success is in your future, and the monetary security will follow. Serving others raises your frequency, and that is something we all should strive to do!

This new business idea that you have is a great one. Perhaps having a business partner that shares your vision will help to propel this idea forward. Stay passionate, and keep manifesting this business in your mind. Do this by saying you already have it, and it is already successful. Envision the business in your mind and its success as though it is happening in the now. Things will begin to unfold.

Sending love and light!!

JUDGEMENT

Today's lesson of the day is not to judge others. We are living in a time where judging others is something human beings do on a regular basis. We look and see how others live their lives, what they do, how much they make, what they look like, their relationship status, their religion, their sexual orientation, gender, where they live, and the list goes on and on.

We are in constant judgement of others whether we would like to admit it or not. No one is excluded from this because it is our ego brain that puts these thoughts into our minds. Ego is the part of our brain that sends off signals of fear, doubt, judgement, anxiety, etc. So, when we meet someone for the first time or see someone on the street, we immediately begin calculating in our heads if we deem that person worthy of our time or not.

When we are judging others, we are often judging a piece of ourselves. It is a mirror. Perhaps it is time to reflect on our judgements. We each have our own individual soul contracts we agreed to before coming here. When you see other people around you, see them as adventurers, just as you are. We are all here in this simulation to learn and grow and oftentimes learn and grow together. Because we are all one.

We are here to learn, love, grow, and remember who we truly are as souls. Everyone is just going about it in a different way. We are all trying to figure it out together. When you look at someone, instead, look at them with love, compassion, and understanding. We are all in this together.

Sending love and light!!

THE JUGGLE

Today's lesson of the day is if you find you are juggling too many things at once, and you are feeling overwhelmed, it is time to take a moment for yourself to regroup and find a place of calm. We have a lot on our plate, and that can feel extremely overwhelming at times. We are only one person with two hands, not eight, and juggling a thousand things at once can raise our blood pressure and give us high amounts of stress and anxiety.

This is your reminder that you need to take care of yourself first. You are running around so much you are forgetting about you. Remember, you are very important to this world, but it is hard to do good in the world if you do not have your full strength and energy. You are finding yourself being drained and you are running on empty. It is time to take a time out from everything, and have a moment for some self-care.

Allow yourself to say, "I need a time out." Go do something that relaxes you. Go get a massage, go read a book, meditate, take a long hot shower or bath, go out to your favorite restaurant, meet up with friends, listen to fun music and dance it out in your room. Whatever makes you the happiest, it is time to do it. This raises your frequency and will give you a clearer head and mindset. We cannot always look to others to fill our cups; we can do it for ourselves by practicing self-care.

Once you do this for yourself, because everyone deserves it, it is time to tackle your list of important tasks one at a time. It is much easier to accomplish one thing at once than a hundred things at once; one thing is much more manageable. Take a breath. You are doing amazing things and you are doing great! Just remember not to forget about yourself and your needs so you can tackle life one step at a time.

Sending love and light!!

HARD WORK IS PAYING OFF

Today's lesson of the day is that you have worked so hard to reach your goals and it is going to pay off. You have been working toward a big goal in your life for some time, and now you must believe everything is going to be possible for you because it is! You have had your challenges, and sometimes you have felt your goals have been out of reach. Keep manifesting positive things by saying that it is already happening in this moment.

Picture yourself already at the finish line and already meeting your goals. That it has already happened right now. Believe it wholeheartedly. You have learned incredible knowledge from your past experiences from both positive and negative events, and this knowledge is going to help you now in your present. Happiness, joy, and fulfillment is coming your way. Trust the process.

Remember that finding your happiness and fulfillment does not mean it will not be challenging, but things will start to lighten up soon. Your thoughts, words you speak, and actions matter, so really focus on staying in a positive mindset and positive frequency whenever possible. Be proud of your battle scars; they tell a story of bravery and resilience and determination. You are a warrior!!

Sending love and light!!

HOPE, ABUNDANCE, AND BALANCE

Today's lesson of the day is that you are entering a time of hope, abundance, and balance. You have been through a lot over the past few months, but you are finally coming into a time of calm. You have been manifesting positive thoughts, and those thoughts of hope have been heard. You will notice your wishes being answered. Some manifesting takes time, so make sure to have patience as well.

When you look around you, you will notice the abundance of love surrounding you, but mostly you will begin to recognize the more important love you have for yourself. Through self-love your light will shine and touch others. Before you can fully love others, we need to love ourselves from the inside out. You are beginning this self-love process, and your light is beginning to shine brighter than before.

Everything is going to start to align. You will feel things begin to settle down, and the chaos will subside. It will be very important, when all of this occurs, to stay in the present moment. Often, once our lives calm down, we fear losing the balance and abundance in our lives. We begin living in the future rather than the present. Take a moment to meditate and ground yourself and come back to the now.

All is working for our highest good whether it feels like it or not. So, trust the process, and know you are deserving of happiness. We are always being guided even when we do not feel we are. It is also the perfect time to make a wish; please do.

Sending love and light!!

YOUR EXCITEMENT IS
YOUR OPPORTUNITY

Today's lesson of the day is to let your passion for something drive you into the opportunity of your dreams. So often, when we are younger, we are taught to be driven more by money than what excites us in life. The thing is, choosing a career based on money will leave you feeling empty and unfulfilled. You will begin to ask yourself the important question, "what is it I truly want?"

Instead of forcing yourself into a career that makes you unhappy, it is time to decide what is right for you. What will fill your soul's purpose? Think back to when you were a child and you had big dreams, what were those dreams? How about when you were a young adult? What excited you? And what are your dreams right now in this moment?

Make a list of everything you are passionate about. Is it creating recipes? Is it animals? Is it music? Is it helping others in some way? As you sit in your cubicle at work, what is the fire inside you saying? Where are you being pulled? We are most fulfilled and happy when we are doing what we are being pulled to do. Deep inside of you, you want more out of life, and now is the time to go for it.

After making a list of everything you are passionate about and excites you, look at the list and see how you can create an opportunity for yourself. If you were given a blank canvas, what would you do with it? Anything and everything is possible if you believe it to be true. Create the experience you want. You have so much passion inside, perhaps it is time to let it loose!

Sending love and light!!

FEARING YOUR INTUITION

Today's lesson of the day is about not fearing your intuitive gifts. When you begin this journey of spiritually awakening, you will notice your frequency rising. When this happens, the veil between this dimension and others becomes thinner, and you may notice some odd changes or shifts that you cannot explain.

You may start to notice more thoughts coming into your head that are not your own. You may start to sense others' energies around you. You may see more clearer images of certain things in your mind about other people that you cannot explain. You may wake up in the middle of the night abruptly, catching your breath as though you have been somewhere else and returned, but at the same time, never left your bed. You may suddenly have a knowing about things you would not normally know about. You may see energies of the past.

Oftentimes, when these things occur, we feel as though we are going crazy. What has actually shifted is our consciousness. You always had intuitive gifts all along, everyone does, they just may not have been strong enough due to the frequency you were in previously. This means that you may have noticed these gifts before, but you were able to explain it away.

Rather than stressing or fearing over these beautiful gifts, it is time to explore them more so you can be the one in charge of your own experience. Understanding is knowledge, and knowledge is power. It is time to explore your Source-given abilities. These intuitive gifts are your birthright. They are meant to remind you of your connection between this dimension and others. Consider it like a cell phone – you can call home while you are away at school. Instead, the cell phone is always free and is always inside of you. Push fear aside! It is time to explore!

Sending love and light!!

TREATING OTHERS FAIRLY

Today's lesson of the day is about treating others fairly and not taking advantage of them. This could mean in relationships, business, anything really. When we consider the fact that we are all one as souls, we must remember that how badly we treat others is harming ourselves. That means that treating others poorly will only harm you in the end.

"Treat others the way you want to be treated." If we look at the law of attraction, our thoughts, words, and actions come back to us in one form or another. The universe is always listening and watching and is always ready to give and receive energy from us. However, the universe does not discriminate and will give back the same energy that it has received. Since actions matter, and you are not treating others fairly and doing inappropriate things, that negative energy will come back to you.

It is time to examine your behavior in your loving relationships and relationships in business. How are you treating others that are around you? Is the way you treat everyone around you the way you would like to be treated now or in the near future? If not, it is time to make a change for the better. All change comes from within. It is a choice. And by choosing to treat others around you better from within, you will notice a difference in how others treat you in return.

Sending love and light!!

FINANCIAL STABILITY

Today's lesson of the day is about coming into financial stability very soon. Recently, you have felt that money has been flying out the door in every direction. Sometimes it even feels as though you are just throwing money away lately. But know that this feeling of loss will begin to shift into a feeling of gain very soon for you.

Adulting is challenging and we can often feel as though we are not in control of our own lives at times. We find ourselves struggling trying to put food on the table and survive. But things are about to change for you. Your fight for stability and security is about to pay off. You have been trying to save money little by little when you were able, and this effort has not gone unnoticed.

You are strong; much stronger than you think because you have accomplished this monetary goal through all the challenges. However, you are going to need to be careful of holding on too tightly to material possessions out of fear. Instead of going into a negative frequency of lacking something, shift your consciousness into a positive frequency of abundance instead.

This is the "glass is half full" mentality. Be thankful for what you do have rather than worrying about what you do not have. This will shift your consciousness in a positive way. Remember positive thinking gets you positive results, where the same goes for negative thinking gives you negative results. Just shifting your way of thinking will make a huge difference in your life. Try it out and see for yourself!

Sending love and light!!

REDISCOVERING YOURSELF

Today's lesson of the day is about rediscovering yourself. You have been through such a difficult time in your life. You have built up walls of protection since you were a child out of necessity. However, those walls were not built on solid ground to begin with. The child-self within you has been locked away in the tower trying to be freed. However, you thought keeping your child-self in the tower would protect them, but instead, it was only a prison.

It is time to let your child-self out of the tower so they can go back to exploring. Our child-selves are our curiosities, our dreamers, our playfulness. At some point as a child, you needed to protect them from external circumstances. But after those threats were over, you never went back to let the child within free. We want so badly to protect our child within, but it is time to let go. Letting go is not always easy on your own.

Meditation and therapy are always a great place to begin. It is time to tear down the walls you have built and rebuild again on more solid ground. A place where your child-self can run free and without fear or judgement. This is also about raising frequency. If you feel you are surrounded by a dark cloud, fill the space around you with positive energy: upbeat music blasting, dancing like a kid again, exercise, walks in nature, meditation, etc.

It is time to look within right now and rediscover the love for yourself that has been missing. Through fully loving yourself without conditions, you will radiate your beautiful light outward, and others around you will see it. You are not hopeless, you are hope. Remember to give yourself compassion and grace through this process. You will soon notice a change!

Sending love and light!!

THE FREQUENCY SHIFT

Today's lesson of the day is about people who come into your life and out of your life so mysteriously and you cannot understand why. People are meant to be in our lives for a specific purpose, and then once we learn what we needed from them, those people tend to disappear. There are reasons for this. The first is because the lesson was learned, and there was no other need for further interaction with the person.

The other is due to a frequency shift. When you are of a certain frequency, you send out that vibration into the world. When this occurs, people of that same frequency will be drawn to you. For example, if you are the type of person who enjoys gossiping about other people and are always in a state of judging others, you will find yourself surrounded by those of that same frequency. Another example is if you are in the frequency of creating, you will find yourself surrounded by other likeminded creators.

This is not a coincidence because energy frequency is everything. Since we are energy, the vibration you are giving off in your regular state of being attracts that of the same vibration. So, as we shift into a higher energy frequency, you will notice those around you, who are not of the same frequency, will either fight to bring you back down to their vibration because the connection was lost, or disappear completely.

As you shift to a higher frequency, remember that being in a higher vibration is a positive thing. Do not allow others to bring you back down again. You will notice that you will begin to be surrounded by other likeminded individuals of the same energy. We are always shifting, always learning, always growing. Remember that this journey is to remind us of who we truly are. Part of that journey involves us continually shifting to higher frequencies to finally remember and understand. Trust.

Sending love and light!!

THE GRATITUDE RITUAL

Today's lesson of the day is about the gratitude ritual. At the human level, we tend to live in the ego mind where we often feel doubt, lack, uncertainty, fear, anger, sadness, anxiety, etc. Though we cannot always stop those emotions from coming when we are in specific moments in our lives, there comes a point when it is time to remember the important things in life that you are grateful for.

Having gratitude every single day is something that will naturally raise your energy frequency, and a higher energy frequency means being in a better place in the mind and heart, which is something we all strive for. The guides suggest this gratitude ritual. This is only one way to remind yourself of everything you are grateful for, so they suggest doing whatever works for you: Write a list of everything you feel you are lacking about yourself internally and your external circumstances.

Then write a separate list of everything you are grateful for internally and externally on another piece of paper. Then take the lacking list, light a candle, and then say something like the following: "This negative list of things I am lacking in my life, and the negative energy it possesses, no longer has power over me. I am taking my power back. By burning this list, I disintegrate its negative power, and I will be free to live a life of gratitude. I now release this burden from my heart."

Then safely set the negative list on fire, set it down on something fireproof, and watch your list of things that you feel you are lacking from disintegrate in front of you. Feel that negative energy dissolving from within you. Then take the gratitude list and place it somewhere you can find it every morning when you wake up, and read it out loud to yourself daily. You will feel that energy shift soon enough!

Sending love and light!!

MOVING FORWARD AFTER TRAUMA

Today's lesson of the day is about making the decision to move forward after a traumatic event. You have been through so much in your life, and you have found that your past has caused you a lot of pain and anxiety. What happened to you was not your fault, but here you are forcing yourself to relive it every single day. You feel you are stuck in a loop that just keeps going around and around.

However, you have the power within yourself to stop this negative cycle that has been playing out in your mind. You have been looking for help outside of yourself rather than looking inward. The hardest lesson is to discover the "why." If everything is happening for us and not to us, what was the purpose of the traumatic event that occurred in your life?

Journaling can be extremely helpful with this discovery. Remove yourself from the experience and look more at the event as an observer than a victim. Why did it have to happen? What positive lesson is embedded in the experience? What was meant to be learned? What knowledge did you gain for the future that could help others? Finding answers to these questions will help you to find understanding which gives you power.

It is time to take your power back. You have given your power away. Once you have your power back, you will be able to see that you are not a victim. You are strong and powerful, and you have that power within you already. Everything you need is already inside of you. And with this knowledge, you will be able to advocate for yourself and for others going through their own traumas. But most of all, it is time to love yourself again. Trust the process.

Sending love and light!!

TOXIC WORK COLLABORATION

Today's lesson of the day is about feeling trapped in a work collaboration and knowing when it is time to get out. You are currently working with someone or multiple people that are bringing you down. You took this job for the money, but ever since you started, you have been asking yourself if the money is worth this toxicity?

You are finding yourself dreading going to work daily because you know you will have to work with and around people that are sucking the life out of you; energy vampires. They take from your cup, but do not give anything back in return. You are also finding that collaborating with these people are making your life miserable because you are doing most of the work. They know you are a hard worker and are taking advantage of you.

Now you are feeling trapped. The money is really good. How could you possibly walk away from this? Maybe you are just supposed to live unhappily like this until you retire? You already know the answer to these questions because this has been on your mind for quite some time. The great thing is that this job is not the only job that can give you comfort. But living in a prison for eight or more hours a day is not something that will serve you.

We often are at work more than being at home enjoying our lives and being social with those we love. This makes our jobs significantly important because we spend most of our lives there. It is time to do something career wise you absolutely love with people you love to collaborate with. Why should we do it imprisoned in a work environment that is filled with toxicity? It is time to prioritize your happiness and fulfillment.

Sending love and light!!

SERVING OTHERS

Today's lesson of the day is to step back for a moment and begin to think of ways that you could serve others around you. Other people have been helping you out a lot lately, and it is time to give back in a beautiful way. This can be with people you know or do not know; either way we are all connected because we are all one. Why serve others? And how can we do that?

Serving others raises our frequency. It makes us feel like we are making a difference in other people's lives because we are, and that makes us feel our best. Remember that serving others does not necessarily mean monetarily. Just looking at someone you do not know and wishing them an amazing day can go a long way. It is about showing your appreciation and care for the fellow brave souls that chose to come here at this exact moment along with you.

We do not know what everyone is going through in their lives, and we may never know, but acts of kindness can uplift someone else who may have been having a difficult day. It is about helping to change the frequency of others around you. It is a beautiful thing how powerful we all are that we can affect someone else's energy like that whether it is in a positive or negative way. It is time to have a more positive effect on others.

To serve others means to do it without expecting anything in return. Even if you do something or say something wonderful to someone else and they do not return the kindness, you have planted an energetic "seed" in their minds; they will think about your kindness later and possibly share that kindness with others, and what a beautiful thing that is!

Sending love and light!!

THE POWER WITHIN

Today's lesson is about looking inside of yourself for your power rather than to others outside of you. As many of us were brought up, we were told to look to others for help and guidance and strength. We were to look to adults, religious figures, politicians, etc. We were taught that we had to look for people with power who could save us.

Here is what everyone with that power does not want you to know: everything you need is already and always has been inside of you. Because everyone and everything comes from Source, we are fractals of it, which makes us all one having this experience. This means the power is already inside you because you are the power, you are already the driving force.

People who love taking power away from others do so to feel important and strong, but at the same time, those people are also giving their power away to others because without others to control, they would have nothing: no strength, no importance, no power. For another example, take religious figures who say they are closest to God, so others must talk through *them*. That is control. How can that be true when God is already a part of you?

You can look to others for guidance if that gives you a sense of security, but when you realize you can give yourself security and guidance, you will see the truth. That you are powerful, strong, smart, and intuitive. The energies of all that is and ever was is inside of you at this moment. That is ancient knowledge that is within you. You are much more powerful than you think you are, and you can access that power at any moment. Trust and believe!

Sending love and light!!

TAKING YOUR TIME WITH YOUR NEW BUSINESS

Today's lesson of the day is about taking your time when it comes to starting your new, exciting business. When we have an incredible idea for a new business, and we are extremely passionate, we often want everything to happen right now this moment. We get extremely impatient, and we try to put the foot on the gas to speed things up. But we must remember to nurture this amazing opportunity.

Think of it like giving birth to a child. You find out you are pregnant, but it is still going to take some time before the baby is ready to be born. It is not a process that can be rushed, it takes time and planning. The same goes for your new brilliant idea. You are in the planning stage of your new business.

Remember to stay in the present. What does your new business look like right now? What steps can you take today? Nurture this beautiful time before the business gets off the ground. Because just like a child, your life is going to change in a beautiful way when the time is right. And since everything is happening for us, trust that your new business will take off when it is supposed to. You will know when.

The planning stage is such an exciting and beautiful place to be. Let your creativity take you to an incredible place of imagination, and trust that you are being divinely guided and inspired. You are going to help a lot of people with this new business, and that is the whole idea for each of us: to serve others in any way we can. Keep the passion, but just make sure not to rush the process, and live in the now. You are on your way! Learn from the journey.

Sending love and light!!

CELEBRATE WHAT YOU HAVE REBUILT

Today's lesson of the day is to celebrate the fact that you have rebuilt your life after losing everything. You have been through so much. You once had it all: the partner, the house, the vacations, the cars, the dogs, the kids, the white picket fence; then, unexpectedly, you lost everything. Perhaps it was through divorce or some other happening that flipped your life upside down.

You did not imagine this for yourself. You were not sure you would be able to get your life back together. Everything seemed confusing and impossible. But one day you decided to take one step forward, and then another step, and then another. You did the impossible. You took control of your life, and instead of relying on someone else, you began to rely on yourself.

You saw that you are and always were more than capable, but it was just too hard to see before. Sometimes we must lose everything and hit bottom before we can rebuild on much sturdier ground. You have learned hard lessons, but they were important. You have become stronger and you have also begun to find your strength and power within. It is about loving yourself fully without conditions first and foremost.

It is time to celebrate you as you rediscover yourself. You have risen from the rubble. And though you have risen scathed, you are healing your wounds and becoming stronger than ever before. And as you continue to rebuild your life, you will notice that you have much more than you had before. That even after all the pain and loss, you are wealthier in so many ways. So, celebrate you; because you are worth celebrating.

Sending love and light!!

YOU ARE CAPABLE OF ANYTHING

Today's lesson of the day is to believe in yourself fully, and that you are capable of anything. When it comes to your job, you have been extremely dedicated. You know exactly what you are doing, and you know it is time to get a promotion. But sometimes you fill your mind with doubts that hold you back.

Your initial reaction to going for a promotion is: This is definitely for me! I deserve this! And a split second later your ego brain pops in saying: But am I really capable? What if I cannot do it? What if I let other people down? Your first reaction of going for the promotion was your gut instinct, your intuition. It is the part of you that knows best. It is the egoic human brain that comes in immediately after with the doubt.

Which do you follow? The ego brain is great at keeping us out of immediate dangers, but your intuition is your inner guide and spirit guides trying to aim you into a certain direction that will help you. If your first reaction is that you are capable of anything, which you are, and deserving, which you are, then it is time to go for it!

Ask yourself why you are afraid to take a chance? What is the worst that could happen? You are smart, hardworking, dedicated, knowledgeable, and the list goes on. It is time to believe in yourself fully. Believe you are deserving because you are. Imagine you already have that promotion in your mind and believe that fully. If we believe in ourselves, others will believe in us. But belief begins within first.

Sending love and light!!

THE BALANCE OF WORK
AND LIFE

Today's lesson of the day is about finding a work and life balance. These days it seems we go to work for most of the day, and then to prove our worth further, we bring work home with us, and work until we go to bed. This means that when you come home, you are not living your life. In fact, are you even living at all?

A job is something we currently must have because that is the collective agreement we have made as human beings. This allows us to have roofs over our heads and be able to afford to have food on our tables. This will not always be the case as the collective continues to shift to higher frequencies. But at this moment, this is what is expected of us to survive.

Our purpose here is to love ourselves and others, serve others in a way that heals and helps to raise the frequency of the collective, learn and grow from all lessons, remember who we are on a soul level, enjoy human connections, but also to find balance in our lives. Without balance we feel off constantly, and this can wreak havoc on our mental and physical selves.

If you are always working, you are not living. And if you are not living, you are not enjoying the true beauties of life. This is your reminder that you need to find that balance. Once you do, you will finally feel a sense of calm that you have been hoping for. It is time to create boundaries, where you are finally having the experience you want to have, and not what society expects from you. What do you want? It is your choice.

Sending love and light!!

THE JUDGEMENT OF OURSELVES

Today's lesson of the day is that we are not judged on the other side, but that we judge ourselves. After we transition from physical form back to our true selves, we go through a life review where we get to watch our lives from the beginning. Did we learn the lessons that we agreed to learn? Did we treat people with love, respect, kindness, and compassion? Did we grow in a positive way after challenging events in our lives? But why go through this life review at all?

Since we are in "school" right now, and Earth is one of the most difficult, densest, and uncomfortable schools, we are here to learn some of the most difficult lessons there are. This means we have all graduated from other schools around the universe and other dimensions, and now we are all trying to get our PhDs here. That is not an easy task, but it is part of our growth.

While we are put through constant tests throughout our lives, when we transition back to our home, it is time for our life review. You go through all the moments of when you brought people joy, and you feel the other person's joy. You also see where you brought people pain, and you feel the way those people felt as well. This is not out of judgement or punishment; this is to teach us so we can be better the next time around.

It is time to see the world differently. Love yourself unconditionally. Love others. Show others kindness and compassion. Help others around you who may need assistance. Remember that we are all here trying to learn the most challenging lessons, so have compassion for the other brave souls who have chosen to upgrade along with you. All we can do is the best we can with the information we have in the moment.

Sending love and light!!

MEDITATION AND DECISION MAKING

Today's lesson of the day is about using meditation to help make decisions. Sometimes we are faced with difficult and challenging decisions. So, how do we know how to choose what is best for us? When we are faced with too many choices, we tend to go into panic mode because we are worried about making the wrong decision. That can feel extremely overwhelming.

It is time to ground yourself and get to a place of calm. Meditation is such an important tool to help with this. However, so many people believe they are incapable of meditation or think they are doing it wrong. Who is to say your way of meditation is wrong? Your way is the only way that matters. You do not have to sit on the ground somewhere with your eyes closed if you are unable to sit still.

You can meditate by walking alone in nature, meditate while gardening, some go running as a meditation as well. There is no one magical way. Meditation calms and grounds you which helps to dissolve the cloudiness in connecting with your inner guide. So, if you are unable to meditate by sitting still, think about the one thing that is calming to you, and connect to your inner self during that activity.

Before meditating, set your intention. What decision are you trying to make? Then begin your meditation, whatever that looks like for you, and listen to your intuition. You will notice the cloudiness in your brain begin to dissipate, and you will start to hear or see the answer you are trying to seek. Trust the information you are given, and know you are always being guided.

Sending love and light!!

THE EARTH SCHOOL TESTS

Today's lesson of the day is about working with your partner to get through negative situations. When we come here to Earth school, we are put through a series of tests; not just as individual souls, but as partnerships, and even collectively. Many times, these tests can include monetary situations. This is why money always seems to be a culprit in arguments or the dissolve of a union between two people.

While living here temporarily, we have agreed to forget who we are on a soul level to learn many lessons fully, however, sometimes the materialistic world can get in the way of our purpose of loving ourselves and loving others. We even equate materialism with our self-worth. If we do that to ourselves, it is no wonder we project that outwards to our partners or others around us.

In our society, we unfortunately judge everyone on what they have monetarily or materialistically rather than who they truly are. That is a lot of pressure, which then filters through our relationships causing tension, stress, anxiety, depression, fear, and anger. How can we stop this egoic materialistic mindset? You and your partner are meant to go through a series of tests together. You are meant to see if you two are strong enough to survive through a world that focuses solely on materialism. But how?

It is time to remember yourselves at a soul level. It is not about the money, the house, the cars, the lavish trips; it is about love, connection, trust, compassion, gratitude, and tolerance of those around you. Work with each other not against each other. Accept the challenges and tests you and your partner will need to face. Always remember the reason you got together in the first place: love. Never forget that.

Sending love and light!!

SHOWING LOVE AND APPRECIATION

Today's lesson of the day is about coming up with ideas to show our partners we love them and appreciate them. Once we have been in a relationship for a long time, we often forget to show our partners how much they mean to us. We can sometimes take them being there for granted, almost like permanent fixtures in the home. But they are much more than that.

The romantic spark has gone for many years now, but that does not mean you cannot get that back. It is time to come up with ways to bring your relationship to how you both felt at the very beginning. It is time to reintroduce yourselves to each other and get to know each other on an even deeper level.

Perhaps you ask each other out for the first time – again. Plan some fun dates together. Just because the spark is gone does not mean it cannot be relit. You both still hold the matches.

In a partnership, it takes two; it is a joint effort, so you both need to be on the same page. Have the conversation with each other. Feel comfortable talking about it because it is important. Trust that your partner will do the work as much as they will need to trust that you will do the same. This could be the start of a new beautiful chapter for you two.

Sending love and light!!

PRIORITIZING SELF-CARE

Today's lesson of the day is about prioritizing self-care when your life feels out of balance. Now, life feels a bit out of whack. You are finding that your stress and anxiety is keeping you up at night or causing headaches that do not seem to go away. When our lives are in an imbalance, it does tend to show up in physical ways in our body as well as in our minds.

As difficult as it seems, we must remember that we have no control over other people. This can be a tough lesson because sometimes we just want to shake a person to make them understand what is best. But that would do nothing in this situation. Unfortunately, that loss of control can give us aches and pains, tightness in the upper neck and shoulder areas causing headaches, among other issues.

The first thing we need to do is understand that we may not have control over others, but we have control over ourselves. So, how do we deal with the imbalance in our lives? Self-care. What are you doing for yourself every day that will bring you to a place of calm and grounding? The guides will always suggest meditation because they consider it such an effective tool. However, self-care can be anything that brings you joy and grounds you.

There are different forms of meditation that do not involve sitting still. Do what feels right to you. Go for walks, get a massage, certain people find cooking relaxing, listen to joyful or relaxing music, working out, etc. Sometimes during tense moments in our lives, we forget about ourselves. However, those are the times we need to take care of ourselves the most. Remember, our external circumstances are often a reflection of the internal.

Sending love and light!!

THE MASTER MANIFESTER

Today's lesson of the day is to explore your abilities as a master manifester and creator. As beings of energy, we are able to create anything we wish to happen through this energy. Here are two important tricks to make this happen.

The first trick is that whatever you want to manifest, you must see it in your mind happening in the now. "I *have* a beautiful home with a two-car attached garage, three bedrooms, filled with love" or another example, "I *have* a loving romantic relationship with a person in my life who is my age, single, emotionally available, trustworthy, kind, and hilarious." Make sure you are as specific as possible. Write down what you want to manifest as well, and read it to yourself before bed and when you get up in the morning. Visualize everything and every detail each time.

The second trick is to believe everything you are manifesting in. Without belief it cannot occur. You cannot manifest certain energy if you do not believe you can manifest it. So, as you read your beautiful manifestation list out loud to the universe every morning and before bed, believe everything you are saying and visualize everything in your mind. It will be so because you say it is so.

We are all master creators. Create. Every experience we have experienced has been created by us to learn specific lessons. Trust the process even when it is the most challenging. Never forget how powerful you are, and never allow anyone to make you believe you are not. The guides cannot wait to see what beautiful things you will manifest in your life!!

Sending love and light!!

GRATITUDE FOR LOVED ONES

Today's lesson of the day is about having gratitude for those family and friends who you love. Your friends and family have been with you through thick and thin, especially when you have been through your most challenging and difficult moments in your life. It is very easy to just say "thank you" and move on. But we have to remember that gratitude is extremely important.

Those folks in your life took time to help you, console you, and would have even given the shirt off their back if you needed. The question is, what have you done for them lately? Life is about give and take. You fill someone's cup, they fill yours. It is a balance of give and take.

If someone is giving too much and the other person is not giving enough, you will find the relationship becoming out of balance. This imbalance can cause negative reactions. All relationships take work, but never forget the gratitude.

Today is a day to call up those people who have helped you through the hard times. Invite them over and make them dinner, plan an outing with them. Do something for them; anything at all. Show your love, gratitude, and appreciation for everything they have done. Give and take, the balance of all relationships. Always remember what you are grateful for and show that appreciation. You will be so glad you did!

Sending love and light!!

SUBSTANCE ABUSE AND FREQUENCY

Today's lesson of the day is about the abuse of substances and how they lower your energy frequency. While we are on our spiritual path, it is so important to be aware of our frequency, and what can affect them daily. This includes what we put in our bodies. In this case, this is about abusing substances like drugs and alcohol.

The higher the frequency, the closer to Source; the lower it is, the harder it is to connect. Consider substances a disturbance in the line of connection. Since we are energy beings, substance abuse lowers your frequency and keeps you there due to this disturbance in the connection. However, it is also important to note, even at the lowest frequency, Source and your spirit team never leave your side, it is just harder to hear them; they are distorted.

As we already know with the law of attraction, what energy you put out comes back to you. Your external world reflects the internal. So, negative energies of the same frequency will have a tendency to latch onto you. This is why, when using substances, negative events continue to happen around the substance user. It reflects what is occurring within them.

As you get off the substances, you will notice your frequency raising again. The disconnection will reconnect and the distortion will dissipate. You will notice the energy surrounding you externally will begin to change in a positive way due to the internal frequency shift. If a person is using substances to forget trauma, that will be the time to heal from it rather than hide from it. There is also no shame in getting assistance from professionals to help you. Trust and believe!

Sending love and light!!

THE CROSSROADS

Today's lesson of the day is about coming to a crossroads in your life where you need to make a choice between going with your passion or staying where you are currently. As we get older, we begin to realize increasingly if we are happy in our current positions or unhappy in them. It becomes more apparent to us. You are sitting at your desk at work every day of the week asking yourself, "is this really it for me?"

But there is a fire inside of you that already knows what you want to be doing instead. It excites you every time you think about it. But then the fear and doubt creeps in telling you that it is not possible. Our intuitions are our gut instincts; they are there to help guide us when we need them. So, why are we so worried about listening to our intuition?

We worry that our passions are just dreams that will never be realized. Because we feel it is not possible, we hesitate, then we doubt, then we forget all about it and go back to sitting at our desks. The reason why you are so passionate is because we are naturally creative beings. Since we are creators ourselves, it is no wonder creating in general excites us.

It is time to make a decision in your life between what feels safe but makes you miserable and what lights your fire and drives you. The choice is yours. Sometimes we need to take big risks to realize our passions and dreams. Write your biggest passion down on paper. Meditate on it every day. Listen to your inner guide that is always there to assist you on your journey. What images do you see or words do you hear? Write them down. Create. Trust. Believe. Perhaps a new exciting opportunity will emerge for you!

Sending love and light!!

TRUSTING YOUR INSTINCTS

Today's lesson of the day is about trusting your instincts about people in your life. Our gut instinct or intuition is such an amazing, natural tool that we use daily. We use it continually in every aspect of our lives, especially when considering those around us the most. This means friends, family members, bosses, co-workers, etc.

Lately, you have been having a sinking feeling in your gut about someone in your life. You feel they are either manipulating you, stealing from you, or being deceitful to you in some way. We do not just think someone is doing us wrong because we have nothing else better to do. This person in question has made your eyes squint, your stomach drop, and you have even felt gaslighted at times.

At first, you thought you were being paranoid, but you know you are not. Something feels off and wrong. You also cannot understand why else your stomach would drop while thinking about this person. Deep down you know they are doing you wrong. This is when we need to lean into our intuition. Your body is giving you signs that something is going on. Our bodies are giving us signs all the time. We need to listen.

However, nothing can be hidden forever. All truths come out eventually. You have been right before by trusting your gut. It is your inner knowing, your inner guide. Try to understand what your body is trying to tell you. Gaslighting is one of the worst forms of manipulation. It makes us doubt our intuition. Take your power back. Trust your gut. You will soon see you were right.

Sending love and light!!

EQUAL DISTRIBUTION

Today's lesson of the day is about equally distributing the weight of responsibility between you and your partner. It is so important to remember that when you enter a relationship, it is also a partnership. Life can be very tough and challenging if all the weight is on one person, and that can begin to cause tension.

At the beginning of a relationship, there is a phase of getting to know someone, and there is a beautiful excitement about that. However, relationships are also about working together and balance. Without balance the scale would tip over one way or the other. As you learn about the other person, you will both see how the two of you can contribute to the partnership.

If one person in the relationship is carrying the entire heavy load themselves, what do you think will occur? No one can carry that weight for long, and the partnership will begin to collapse. Resentment comes into play, and anger and frustration being held within will start to come out towards the other person. So, how can we prevent this from happening?

Communication is the key. Without it, a partnership can never be sustainable. A relationship is a delicate flower that needs to be nurtured. Communication and love is the water necessary for the flower to grow. If one of you in the relationship is carrying too much on your own, have that discussion together. Help each other carry the weight. Be there for each other. Work together to achieve that important balance, and you will soon see that you are both a beautiful team.

Sending love and light!!

THE NEW BIG CHAPTER

Today's lesson of the day is about a new big chapter beginning for you. You have been through a lot these last few years. You have had to do so much healing during this time, and it has felt incredibly challenging. You have also had to rediscover yourself. And now, after all this time, you are moving into the next chapter of your life. It almost feels like a rebirth.

You understand now that you had to go through everything in your past to get to this incredible place in the now. Without the pain, you would not have seen the path that you see at this very moment. There is a plan for you, even when you have felt that you had been forgotten. But no one is forgotten, and there is a special purpose and reason for everything that occurs in your life.

Today begins this new chapter, this new journey, this new adventure. You are not even remotely close to the same person you used to be. You are a stronger more confident you. You have learned to love yourself more. And even though loving yourself is a continuous journey, you are here for it. You are showing up for yourself more than you ever have before. What an incredible time for you.

Trust in the process, and know that there are no coincidences. Now that you are beginning this new chapter in your book of life, make sure to live in the moment rather than worry about the future. As you can see from your past that any challenges you will face are for a purpose. Embrace challenges. Continue to find ways to love yourself and others. Enjoy this new and beautiful you. Let this new journey begin.

Sending love and light!!

THE HINTS

Today's lesson of the day is that our mind and body are at their most calm state when following our passions. Our bodies and our minds are always giving us hints. They tell us if what we are doing at any given moment is serving us or not.

When following our bliss, we find that the world seems calmer, brighter, more aligned. Everything feels possible. This is a time when we feel at our healthiest and best. However, when we are not following our bliss, we find that we are agitated, stressed, angry, susceptible to headaches or migraines, and unable to sleep.

Here is the kicker: to follow our bliss, it often takes a massive leap of faith. It involves taking risks. And for many people, the fear takes over and we go with what is safe. We suddenly feel like we are only human, and our bliss seems to float further away.

But remember that we are much more than human. We are extremely powerful souls. We are capable of everything and anything because we are creators. We are brilliant manifestors. We can literally make anything happen. Remember who you really are because there is more power there than you could ever imagine.

Sending love and light!!

PATIENCE, PLEASE

Today's lesson of the day is about having patience as beautiful things in our life grow. We are an "I want it now" type of society. We expect it in our relationships, our careers, our lives in general. But there are reasons for everything, and one of the number one reasons is that it is not the right time.

We get things in life when it is the right moment to get them. If you got into a certain relationship too soon, perhaps you would not have appreciated it as much as you would in the future. Or if you met someone before it was time, you may not have been in the right state of mind to be able to handle a relationship.

The same goes for our work life. We want things to be done right away, but perhaps it did not get done right away so that a specific outcome would occur. If everything is happening for us and not to us, why did things turn out the way they did? It is a good idea to reflect and see how everything in your past was lined up perfectly to get you to this moment. You can start to see the outline of your soul's plan.

It is now time to learn patience. We need to take a moment to reflect, and know that everything is playing out the way it is supposed to; to get you to your next destination. If the waters of life are feeling stagnant at the moment, just know you are just waiting until a rush of water comes to push you forward. Wonderful things take time. Trust in the process.

Sending love and light!!

YOUTHFUL ENTHUSIASM

Today's lesson of the day is to explore new opportunities with youthful enthusiasm rather than with a jaded mindset. As we get older and wiser and have more experiences, we tend to have very strong opinions about life in general. In many ways, due to the challenges life throws at us, we can often become jaded as time goes on.

This is not only opportunities in career, but also relationships. For instance, it is very easy to bring past baggage with you into another relationship. You know it is a new person with new possibilities, but something in you, possibly past relationship trauma, causes you to be cynical about the new connection. There is also a possibility that you believe all people are the same as the ones you have encountered.

In a career, if you have always seemed to work with negative people, you automatically begin to assume the next job will be the same. It is so important to be careful what you think because thoughts are energy. The law of attraction is always there and will always be, so be careful how you approach a new opportunity. If you think it will be terrible, it will be because you say it is so.

It is time to approach new relationships and new job opportunities with a youthful spirit. Have that excitement, that wonder. That anything and everything is possible because it is. See the beauty in every new possibility without bringing along the baggage. If you have baggage to carry, perhaps it is time to invest in a professional therapist who can do EMDR (Eye Movement Desensitization and Reprocessing) therapy to help you move forward. There is never any shame for needing the extra help.

Sending love and light!!

GROUNDING

Today's lesson of the day is about grounding yourself and coming back to center during moments of chaos. The guides first showed a tornado and then a hurricane. Each circling and spiraling and twisting. Natural chaos in the world. Each with a calm center point.

These images are symbols showing that our peace and calm is within each of us, even when chaos is constantly around us. We must remember to go back to our center. To ground ourselves. To get to that peaceful center where we can breathe, collect our thoughts, find understanding, and have clarity.

Life is very much a chaotic sequence of events, and many times we get wrapped up in it. We feel a part of it. Often, we feel we cannot escape the chaos. But that is not true. By centering ourselves and grounding ourselves, we are able to get to the stillness. It is our eye of the storm. It is the peace we are searching for when we need it most.

How can we ground ourselves? Meditation, gentle vagus nerve stimulation, listening to soothing music, taking drives in less populated areas, long walks in nature, working out, etc. There are many ways to ground ourselves and come back to our center; our peaceful place within us. When you are in a storm, acknowledge it, give yourself grace, and begin to find the peace from within; there is healing in the stillness.

Sending love and light!!

OBSTACLES ARE LESSONS

Today's lesson of the day is about every day obstacles in life that are meant to teach lessons. You get caught up in a traffic jam or a construction site on the expressway, and they are holding you back. You sit there seething and frustrated. You get more and more upset and begin to yell and scream profanities as you slam your steering wheel. You notice the traffic is now worse. In fact, now there is an accident up ahead.

It is time to dial back a moment, take a breath, and understand that there is a great possibility that you are being taught one of the most difficult lessons to learn in these human vessels we are currently in: patience. Patience feels impossible when you are running late, your blood pressure is high, and your steering wheel is getting an unnecessary beating.

But think for a moment that this is actually a lesson you need to be taught. If this was a test, would you be passing the exam or getting a "needs improvement"? Many of us, when it comes to patience, fall into the "needs improvement" category. This is not a judgement, just a fact. You can tell by all the angry drivers whizzing by you, honking horns, screaming obscenities, and using questionable hand gestures at others.

If everything we are working through in our lifetimes are lessons, patience is one of the biggest and often most difficult. Sit there, take three deep breaths (in for a 4 count and out for a six count). This will lower your frustration level. Feel the anger dissipate. More frustration and anger and stress will only make the matter worse. Do not do that to yourself. It is time to learn this valuable lesson.

Sending love and light!!

BASK IN THE GLORY

Today's lesson of the day is to enjoy your current joy, success, and the fulfillment you have had recently. What a beautiful day for you! Everything is in alignment today, and all things seem to be in harmony. Today you woke up with nothing but joy and excitement in your heart. So, what is the lesson in that? To live for today. Live in the moment. It is important not to say, "things are going well; something negative is going to happen now."

Stay in this beautiful moment. Life is challenging enough as it is, but we are meant to not only go through challenging moments, we are also meant to go through incredible and fulfilling, joyful moments. It is a day to feel that love around you. Go outside in nature and listen to the birds singing and celebrating life with you. How will you celebrate this joy today?

There are wonderful lessons in living for the moment. And all lessons are important to learn. So, if you are a person who generally takes a fantastic moment and shadows it with negativity, perhaps this is the time to learn the lesson to acknowledge them, and then let those thoughts leave your mind. Imagine the negative thoughts (which are just energy) exiting or dissolving in your mind. Then concentrate on your heart chakra. Picture the beautiful ball of light inside and imagine it expanding outward. Close your eyes and think of three things you are grateful for and smile.

Feel that warmth and that love. This is an incredible moment. Take it all in and celebrate it! You are worth it! Trust and believe!!

Sending love and light!!

CELEBRATE YOUR EFFORTS

Today's lesson of the day is about celebrating your efforts because you are about to see the benefits of your hard work! You have been working towards an important goal for some time, and before today you have not seen a lot of reward. But all of that is about to change. Incredible things are coming. Believe it and trust the process.

Timing is everything. Before we came to this planet for another semester of Earth school, we agreed upon certain events happening throughout our lives. But here is the kicker, these events need to happen at the precise time they are meant to. True, we all have free will to get from point A to point B, but point A and point B are set. There can just be multiple ways to get there.

So, if point A and B and so on are set in our soul contracts, that means that big moments in our lives have been planned out already. And if you want to get even more mind blowing, your past, present, and future are all happening at the exact same time. But thinking about that will only make our minds hurt. The point is that large moments are already planned out for us, and they will not happen until they are supposed to.

This is now the time when things are going to change for the better for you. It will because it is the right specific moment for it to occur. Because it is written. Life is meant to have its ups and downs, and you are entering a positive phase. You deserve all the happiness and fulfillment you are about to experience. Celebrate this moment!

Sending love and light!!

PARENTHOOD

Today's lesson of the day is about parenthood, and the stress parents put on themselves. You are beginning to bring up or have brought up children in your life. You were nervous you were going to do something wrong. You put a lot of pressure on yourself because of that fear. It is not easy shaping the youth of the world, but here is something important you should know.

Although you have some influence on how your child thinks, what they believe, and their actions, they are still individuals who have their own soul mission and important lessons to learn. We cannot stop children younger or older from learning important life lessons their souls came here for. As the guides have mentioned, each soul creates a soul contract before coming. During the creation of this contract, major "plot points" are created. Though we all have free will, those major plot points must be realized.

358

This should take some pressure off your shoulders. Your child chose to be born to you for a reason depending on the lessons they have chosen to learn. This does not mean that you should not have considered raising children as a huge responsibility, because it is. But when it comes to molding and shaping your children, you are meant to do the best you can with the knowledge that you have, and then they take over the rest.

The guides understand that you want to protect your children at any age, but eventually the baby birds need to fly out of the nest. You will always be there for advice and guidance when needed. As your child tries to discover themselves and who they want to be, their beliefs will also change as they explore their own truth. Again, it is what their soul wishes to learn in this lifetime. It is time to understand it is not all on you.

Sending love and light!!

TRAVELING

Today's lesson of the day is about the excitement of traveling and learning about different cultures and new ideas. It is time to get out of town for a few days to go enjoy what the world has to offer. There is so much to see and learn and experience. You are currently feeling a bit stuck and a bit uninspired lately, but that is because the scenery you have been around has not changed.

Where do you want to go? What do you want to see? And if this is about money, you do not have to spend a lot of money to have a change of scenery. What is your idea of a getaway? Is it hiking in nature? Is it being next to water? Is it feeling like a child again and going on rides? Is it sampling new foods of the world? Is it a spa weekend with complete relaxation? Is it driving from location to location with friends or family?

Seeing the same things every single day can make life feel a bit stale. This is completely normal. Because we are creative beings at our cores who love soaking in new ideas and new places. We are students of life, so we must learn and experience. So, if you have not planned a moment to steal away from life for a moment, it is a great time to do it!

Life is complicated and challenging, and this is going to refill your cup which really needs to be filled at the moment. Even if it is just for the weekend. Remember that life is one big orchestrated play, and to keep things interesting, there are often set changes. You are the creator of this play. What will the next scene change look like? Just imagine and make it happen! You deserve it!!

Sending love and light!!

A COLLABORATIVE SHIFT

Today's lesson of the day is about an important collaboration you are involved with. When you first began this opportunity together, you were on the same page. You had the same goals, the same dream, the same everything. This is what drew you together in the first place. It felt right, and you took the leap.

However, you are starting to see a strange shift in your partner that you did not see before. They are starting to have other ideas you do not agree with, or they are beginning to act as though they are trying to take over. This is when communication is key, and you have been afraid to have this discussion with them because you always try to stay away from conflict or uncomfortable interactions.

When was the last time you sat down to share your current visions? When was the last time you had a heart-to-heart discussion about what you all created? Just as people change throughout time, ideas and dreams shift and change. This is normal. Nothing can really stay the same because everything is constantly evolving. Two things are possible here. Either a compromise can be made or perhaps this partnership has run its course.

It is time to have the important discussion about the "vision." What brought you together in the first place? And why have things shifted? Listen to each other. Hear each other out. See if you can still find some common ground. If you are both in completely different places, you will feel the answer within you. Listen to your intuition, your gut instinct. You will feel your answer within.

Sending love and light!!

THE ROUGH PATCH

Today's lesson of the day is that your relationship is currently going through a rough patch, but things will get better soon. Both of you have said things you regret. You know each other so well, you know what pushes the other person's buttons. The question is, why did it have to go that far? Why did both of you result in hurting each other's feelings rather than having a discussion instead?

Communication is everything. Without it, a relationship cannot exist. There are relationships where people are nervous to say what is on their minds. They should accept you for who you are inside, not what they expect you to be. And the other way around is true as well. You must accept your partner for who they truly are.

Relationships are hard work, but they are also rewarding if you are communicating well. This disagreement you both had occurred because neither one of you wanted to listen to the other. Because you believe you are right or vice versa. But what if you are both right? What if there is a compromise where you could both meet somewhere in the middle?

Once you communicate with each other, you will find the rough waters will begin to calm down. It is time for you both to open your minds and really listen to each other respectfully. Your relationship will begin to shift in a much more positive direction. This is possible for you both if you truly want it.

Sending love and light!!

YOU ARE A CREATOR

Today's lesson of the day is about how we are all creators and creative beings. At a soul level, we are creators. That is why we are here; to have experiences and to create. Before we came to Earth school you had already created your soul plan. So, at your core, you have always been and will always be a beautiful creator.

This is why you feel so unfulfilled sitting at a desk job for eight or more hours a day. Because you are not doing what you should be doing. This unfulfilled feeling within you then causes you to have bouts of depression and anxiety because you are being forced to "perform" at a high level without using your creativity or your light. This is also why you dread having to wake up early to go to work.

You are meant to shine your light, create, inspire, and dream. Remove those things and you are left with emptiness. It is no wonder you are miserable. You are your own artist in life. If you had an empty canvas to paint, depicting your dreams, what would you paint? Then ask yourself why you stopped yourself from going for it? The answer is usually fear, doubt, and uncertainty.

When you have fear, doubt, and uncertainty, you cannot possibly create in that kind of internal environment. It is time to replace those feelings with fearlessness, confidence, and certainty. Once you believe in yourself fully, you will see that others around you will believe in you as well. Our external world mirrors our internal world. Look within; you have everything within you that you need to thrive.

Sending love and light!!

THE MONEY FEAR

Today's lesson of the day is to not allow fear and doubt help in making important decisions in your life. Let us start with dreams first. Dreams are a high frequency energy. They are usually filled with passion, creativity, love, and excitement. They are what light the pilot light within us. However, fear and doubt are very low frequency energy. They often stop us from getting what we truly want, thus eradicating that fire.

What is one of the biggest fears, if not the biggest fear that often holds us back from our dreams in the physical world? Money. We have given these pieces of paper extreme power over us, and we truly put it on a pedestal above us. We say things such as, "I would love to, but it is too much money." What if money was no object? Would you go for your dreams then?

It is time to believe that those pieces of paper are not above you. You are the one on the pedestal and money sits beneath you; because it is true. So, what are you supposed to do? If starting a business of some kind excites you and has always been your dream, you simply need to do it. Where there is a will there is always a way. Begin by writing down your dream. Imagine in your head that you already have the money and that money is not an obstacle.

What does your dream look like? What is your business plan? What does your working environment look like? Plan it all out. This is manifestation. The universe will give you what you say is true. Without fear or doubt, create your new career. Believe and trust in it. Push fear and doubt aside. You will suddenly see things begin to align with your dreams rather than your fears and doubts. No more holding yourself back; no more fear. Trust and believe.

Sending love and light!!

THE RELATIONSHIP HISTORY

Today's lesson of the day is about your being afraid to tell your new partner about your past relationship history. This lesson is a common fear. Life is about living; and through living, we have experiences. Not all experiences were pleasant and perfect and beautiful. We are meant to have positive and negative experiences.

Perhaps you are not happy about the way you treated someone in a past relationship or how they treated you. But did you learn from it so history is not repeated? This part of your history shows that you can make mistakes, take responsibility for them, and understand the need to change for the future. However, if you have not learned anything and you feel you did nothing wrong, that is another story.

We first must understand that we are not perfect. We can never be perfect. We have always and will continue to make mistakes. All we can do is make decisions based on the information that we know at that time. Sometimes our decision causes a negative effect. You need to forgive yourself. Self-forgiveness is one of the most important things to do for our own growth, especially when trying to move on.

It is time to be open about your past with your future partners. Communication is everything. Perhaps the other person will relate to you on a deeper level. If the other person does not understand, then maybe they are not the right one for you after all. We cannot change history, but we can learn from it, and if someone else is not willing to understand, then at least you know early on. No more hiding or having anxiety over your history because it is how you became the person you are today. No more fear.

Sending love and light!!

YOUR TRUE DESIRE

Today's lesson of the day is about following what you truly desire and dream about deep within rather than being guided by superficial, surface level thoughts created by external societal standards and expectations. Throughout our lives we want to be accepted, so we often will go with the majority so that we are not left behind. This means that we change who we are on the surface so that we can blend in with society.

But we are more than what we are on the surface. Much more. Doing what others expect of you will only make you unhappy and unfulfilled. Why follow when you can lead? Be your own person, the person you are inside. What are your dreams and your desires? What do you want out of life? You get to choose. Society does not get to choose for you.

We are taught daily what society expects from us. How to behave, how to dress, how to think, how to look. Why do we allow ourselves to give in and put on such a facade? Out of fear of acceptance. We want others to accept us so we shove the true and authentic us deep inside and hide there so no one can find us.

But you deserve better than that. The real and true you deserves better than that. You are a leader, a creator, and a dreamer. No one can take that away from you; only you can take that away from yourself. It is time to give yourself permission to be your authentic self now. The person who needs to accept you for you, is you.

Sending love and light!!

LOOK BEFORE YOU LEAP

Today's lesson is about taking time when you have new ideas to think things through rather than jumping in head first without a plan. Patience is key here. All good things take time, and there is so much excitement surrounding new ideas, but make sure you really take a moment to plan things out. New ideas are gifts, enjoy the possibilities.

Why is patience so difficult? Because we are an "I want it now" type of society. However, we cannot get everything now because either it is not the right moment for it to happen or you have not fully considered everything involved yet. Meditate on the idea. Ask your higher-self for guidance. Take notes on what you see or hear or feel. What is your higher-self telling you?

Bringing new ideas to life takes time, and patience can be a long road. But patience is necessary on this new path. Enjoy the process. Often there are lessons built in within the journey itself. These lessons will help you to propel forward. Take a breath, take a pause, and think everything out. You always have amazing ideas, and it will be exciting to see where this takes you.

Trust the process, trust your intuition, and listen for the guidance within. This is a message to look before you leap so you can build your new idea on solid ground rather than on something unstable. You got this!

Sending love and light!!

WHEN IT RAINS, IT POURS

Today's lesson of the day is about the phrase, "When it rains, it pours." When we say this, it is usually because a negative stream of events is occurring at or around the exact same time. Why do negative events come one after the other? The question can also be said for positive events. When the sun is shining, it often shines brighter. Why does the energy remain the same either positive or negative around the same time?

Energy. If something negative occurs in your life, the energy frequency within you becomes lower. It is just a natural progression because it is hard for us not to react to certain situations. We put a lot of energy into specific outcomes which causes us to have frustration and disappointment or sadness and anger due to not getting what we were hoping for. When this energy is radiated off you, it attracts energy of the same frequency right back to you.

This means that other negative energies create other negative events and so on until there is a change in your frequency. So, how can we stop the rain from pouring? Changing our frequency. Which first means lowering our attachments to a specific result or outcomes, and not letting it affect you to the point of lowering your frequency; remembering that everything is happening for a reason. Everything is happening for us not to us.

Meditation helps with raising frequency and keeps you grounded and centered. Gratitude also raises frequency. Say everything that you are grateful for around you. Another way is to blast some upbeat, fun music, and sing and dance your heart out until you feel the positive shift within you. This is about shifting your way of thinking, and you will see a change. Radiate the energy you wish to receive, and you will see things shift in a positive direction.

Sending love and light!!

YOU ARE A HIGHLY
ADVANCED BEING

Today's lesson of the day is that the only possible way for you to be here on Earth is because your soul was ready for the experience. Living here on Earth is challenging. There are wonderful things that happen to us, yes, but this is an extremely low-density planet; so low vibrationally, that souls must be prepared.

The many lives you have already lived on other planets, other dimensions, having been beings of all kinds, has led you to this moment when you were finally ready to begin your next set of lives on Earth. It is the most complicated and complex place to learn. By choice, you are thrown into low energy frequency situations, work and live with others who do not match your frequency causing negative events to occur, relearn self-love, and try to remember who you are at a soul level after being forced to forget.

However, through these challenging circumstances, we learn the most important and most powerful lessons of them all. Empathy, unconditional love for ourselves and others, compassion, and gratitude in its highest form. This is how our souls level up and fully ascend. Yes, this is painful and challenging and uncomfortable. But through all of this, we are also meant to learn to rise above it all.

We are warriors. The other side applauds us because we chose to come here and become our highest possible selves at a soul level. Not all souls are ready for this experience. It is only a select few. *You* got into the school as challenging as it is; you were selected. This is why you have such a big team on the other side. We all need the support. So, get out there, warrior! You got this! The only way you could have gotten here is because you were ready for it!

Sending love and light!!

DIMENSIONAL SHIFTING

Today's lesson of the day is about dimensional shifting and that we do it constantly throughout the day. We are much more powerful beings than you could ever imagine. We are multidimensional. We can shift with our energy frequency. As we shift within ourselves, our external world shifts with it. You just do not realize it is happening; or do you?

For example: you are driving down the road, a car is driving closely behind you, you see it in your rearview mirror. You look up a second later, and the car is gone. The car had no place to turn. Where did it go? Another example: you pass a woman jogging down the street, you look up and the woman is gone. Where could she have gone? She was jogging on a sidewalk in your direction. A final example: you are driving on the road, the vehicle next to you is dark gray, then you turn back and it is the same vehicle except it is now red. No other cars around.

Dimensions do not have to look like different places; they can be versions of the same place with the same people just a different frequency. It is the same thing when you see a dead spider carcass on the floor, you leave it, come back the next day and it is gone, come back the day after and it is back in the same place. The spider carcass only existed in one of the dimensions you were hopping through throughout the day, it simply did not exist in another.

So, what are you supposed to do with this information? Nothing. It happens as you keep shifting frequencies, going back and forth throughout the day. It is natural. But it is fun to notice when you are aware of it. Next time, when you see something and suddenly it is gone or changes, know that is not a coincidence. You simply and effortlessly shifted. Just another thing that makes you one powerful being!

Sending love and light!!

YOU ARE READY

Today's lesson of the day is about being emotionally ready for a relationship that you may have not been ready for before. You have grown so much in the past year and have been through a lot emotionally, and now that you have grown, you are now ready to begin this next step. Emotional maturity is so important, and you may not have appreciated this new relationship if you were not ready.

Your past relationships have not been very healthy, and they may have even caused some anxiety and stress. You also wonder why you had to go through those painful experiences to begin with. Lessons come in all forms; the guides encourage you to look back at past events and see how and why things occurred. Stepping back and looking at things from your past as an observer can shine a light on past issues so that you do not repeat them again.

As much as we want to point fingers at the other people in our lives who have done us wrong, we need to also look within and take responsibility for our part in everything. Think of it like a puzzle. What pieces were necessary on both ends for the event or events to occur? How could the event have been avoided? What would you have done differently? Reflection is so important because self-reflection and self-awareness are our teachers.

Now you are entering a new and beautiful relationship with so many possibilities. You have lived and you have learned. The lessons you have been taught are always with you. Like everyone else, you deserve happiness, so go into this new relationship with an open heart and an open mind. Things will be different this time because you do not *need* a relationship, you *want* one instead, which gives you your power back; and that is a beautiful thing.

Sending love and light!!

STOP ANTICIPATING THE NEGATIVE

The lesson of the day is to stop waiting for and anticipating a negative impact to occur in your life. It is as though you are preparing for an accident or negative event that has not happened. This occurs when positive things are happening all around you, and you feel deep down that something bad is bound to happen sooner or later. It is time to shift your focus so that you do not manifest something negative.

This feeling of negative anticipation is like an anxious driver. Every time they get into a car, they feel that it is the day that they are going to get into an accident. However, having these negative thoughts causes the body to tense up, and this could really cause an accident of your own doing. You are subconsciously manifesting something negative to happen by putting so much power into the scenario.

What do you do when you start to feel that feeling of dread? Feel the feelings, then release them. Do not hold that in. Acknowledge and release. Take deep breaths in and imagine a ball of negative, uncomfortable energy gathering within you, and as you blow it out, imagine the ball of negative energy flowing out of your body.

Do this until the sinking feeling dissipates, then listen to upbeat music or do something that brings you joy to counteract how you felt a moment before and move forward. Meditating also helps. It is all energy, and you are powerful enough that you can do whatever you want with it; use it for your own good.

Sending love and light!!

UNDERSTANDING YOURSELF

Today's lesson of the day is that you do not need to understand someone else's life or their preferences, you only need to focus on your own. As human beings, we tend to be more interested in gossiping about other people or judging them based on how they present themselves in their appearance or their personal lives and preferences. This judgment is often because we feel insecure about something from within us.

Why do you care so much? How is that person affecting you? Do you really admire their confidence because perhaps you are not as confident within? Ask yourself why that judgement came into your mind to begin with because judgement usually occurs due to something happening inside of you that you have shoved deep down into your shadow-self.

Have you made fun of other people in the past? Ask yourself why you did it to begin with. Why did you behave that way? The other person clearly stirred something up inside of you. It often has nothing to do with that other person at all, but it often has everything to do with you. Life is a mirror. What we see in the mirror is reflected back to us. If you feel anger or hatred towards another, it is usually because of anger or hatred you feel for yourself.

It is time to do the inner work and reflect on the questions above. There is always a "why?" Focus on yourself and see if there is something to learn from those other people. Do you wish you were as confident? Did you wish you could be less afraid of being exactly who you are? Are you feeling stifled as a human being because of your fear of rejection from others? The answers to these questions are the keys to your understanding the inner you.

Sending love and light!!

THE INTUITIVE SCARE

Today's lesson of the day is about being aware of people who will try to scare you from developing your intuitive gifts. There are those who will try to scare you into not exploring those Source-given abilities that everyone possesses. It could be due to their own experiences, but they will attempt to make you second guess yourself. It has probably already happened to you while trying to explore and question.

When asking other people for advice on how to grow your own gifts, the answer you should receive is one of helpfulness; not fear, dissuasion, and making you doubt yourself. Your intuitive gifts are your birthright and everyone has them, and no one has the right to tell you that you cannot utilize them. Building your intuitive gifts is like trying to build your muscles at the gym, they will not grow if you do not work them out. To become more confident in your gifts, you need to practice.

Helpful advice should be positive and encouraging. They should be helping you move towards your goals, not away from them. And with the positive advice they are giving you, they should then explain how to do it safely. Just like lifting weights. If you lift heavy weights with poor form, you can ultimately harm yourself unintentionally. When being given advice, ask yourself: are they leading with fear? Is what they are saying helpful to you or making you feel discouraged? Does it support your journey or hinder it? Does their advice serve you?

When working with your intuitive abilities, it needs to be approached in a positive, open, and exciting way. These gifts cannot work when bogged down with fear, stress, and doubt. It is only when we are in a higher frequency that we can truly connect. Your intuitive gifts will always be a part of you. Explore them.

Sending love and light!!

CHILDHOOD TRAUMA HEALING

Today's lesson is about beginning to heal from traumatic childhood events so that you can truly be free from the pain you have been holding onto all these years. It is time to give the child-self within love, compassion, and understanding. This does not mean what happened to you as a child was okay. It is that you are releasing this intense pain from within so that you can move forward.

You have tried to deal with this before, but perhaps it just was not the right time. Today is a different story. You deserve this peace in your life because you have not felt at peace for so long. In fact, you have been projecting your past onto others which is affecting the relationships around you. So, how can you begin to move forward? Remember it is a process.

Everyone heals differently, and there are numerous ways to begin this process. One is speaking with a professional. Make sure you find someone you truly connect with. Another option is a letter burning ritual where you write a letter to those involved in the pain expressing all that you are feeling, read it aloud, and safely burn it saying an affirmation releasing your anger moving forward in peace. Feel that negative energy dissolve inside as the letter disintegrates.

Another option is writing to your child-self. If you were to meet your child-self and discuss past events, what would you tell them? What advice would you give them? What advice would they give *you*? Give your child-self validation and hope. Always lead with love. Explain that what occurred was not your child-self's fault; they were not to blame. Journaling helps us to connect deeper with our inner parts. You are strong. You will move forward.

Sending love and light!!

YOU ARE NOT RESPONSIBLE FOR OTHERS' ACTIONS

Today's lesson of the day is that someone you know is suffering from addiction, and you need to understand that you are not responsible for their actions. You are a very caring person; you have a lot of empathy for those around you. But sometimes reaching out and helping someone does not always work. The person still seems to be tail spinning no matter what you do for them.

The reason this is, is because they do not want to deal with the root cause of the addiction. There is a lot of childhood trauma that they are dealing with that had caused the need to numb the pain rather than face their pain head on. What they do not understand is that they need to run *through* the pain to come out of it rather than running *from* it. Easier said than done.

Now you have made it your responsibility to help this person because you believe you can save them from themselves. However, each time you reach out your hand to them, it seems as though the issue is getting worse. There is a reason why they have been kicked out from place to place and helping hand to helping hand, and now you can begin to understand.

This person you are trying to help needs to make a very important decision. They need to make the decision to help themselves and finally deal with their pain rather than avoid it. But it is a decision only they can make. And as much as you try to save them from themselves, the only person that can save them is *them*. You are not responsible for what they are doing to themselves. You need to release this energy for yourself because it is causing you a lot of stress and anxiety, and that is doing harm to your wellbeing. It is time for that release.

Sending love and light.

FINANCIAL STRESS

Today's lesson of the day is that you are feeling stressed and anxious over your current financial situation, and you are unsure of when it will end. You have bought a new home, and you knew it was going to be a tad uncomfortable monetarily for a bit, but you knew it would be an important purchase for your future. You budgeted everything out, and planned for everything, but you are still feeling worried.

What you are feeling is normal. It can be scary investing in something so important to you. You worry if you can make it happen, worry something will go wrong, worry you made the right choice. But you did make the right choice; you know that. You have done everything up to this point to make your dreams come true. Look what you have accomplished. Look around you; you made this happen, and it is beautiful. Whether you did it alone or with a partner, you have created something special.

You have created a place where there is love and laughter. A place where family and friends can sit together and share stories and memories. A place where board games are played, and food is enjoyed. However, this feeling will not last forever. You will get into a rhythm. And everything that felt difficult for you will begin to get easier. It is always the beginning that can feel the most stressful.

Acknowledge those feelings, but also acknowledge the feelings of love and fulfillment you are also feeling at the same time. The uncomfortable feelings will dissipate, but the beautiful feelings will always be there. There is a reason you are exactly where you are at this moment. It is a journey. What are these feelings and emotions teaching you currently? Why are you meant to feel them? At the end of the day, end with gratitude, because you have more than a lot of people have. Gratitude is so important.

Sending love and light!!

BETRAYED BY A LOVED ONE

Today's lesson of the day is that you have been betrayed by someone very close to you, and now you fear you do not know who to trust. This person is either a family member, a partner, or a friend. This person gained your trust over time, and you felt safe enough where you could let your guard down. But now the person has shown their true colors and you do not know if you can trust anyone again.

First, acknowledge those feelings within. Our minds immediately want to rationalize, saying that it was not that bad. Or maybe you feel like the person will change. Validate yourself that you know exactly what happened. There is healing energy in knowing the truth. Feel all the feelings of sadness, anger, etc.

Journaling helps us find clarity. What signs did you see before that you may have ignored? We naturally want everything to remain the same because it is easier. So, looking back, what can you recognize as being red flags? Perhaps you can learn from this. This does not mean to become paranoid of everyone around you. If that is happening, you have more work to do on your healing.

You also need to give yourself grace. Do not beat yourself up over feeling all the feelings that are coming up. Healing takes time, and it is different for everyone. Perhaps this is a lesson in trusting your intuition, your gut instinct. If something feels wrong or off to you, something probably is. We can always tell a regular day from one that feels strange and off. It is time to trust in that inner guidance.

Sending love and light!!

RELIGIOUS DISCONNECT

Today's lesson of the day is about disconnecting from old religious views because you are seeing the cracks in the system. You have been brought up in a certain religion. It was not a choice; you simply followed what your family members were practicing. As children, we needed to be shown the way because we were always looking for guidance. However, as you grew up, things did not seem to add up. Religion began to stop making sense, but you still believed in something more.

You enjoyed certain traditions that made you feel joyful and grateful, but most of the time you felt disinterested and not wanting to participate. Sometimes this feeling caused you to act out in some way. It also felt like most people, yourself included, were just going through the motions of what was expected of them. They were just there because they felt they had to be.

Another thing you could not understand is that if God or Source was an unconditionally loving being, why was God so vengeful, spiteful, and damning people to fiery torment? You tried so hard to understand, but instead of understanding, you became fearful instead. You were told to trust religious leaders, but their messages of love always seemed to include a message of fear: do this or else!

After doing your own spiritual research, you have found that fear is a low frequency that helps people of power keep others in line. That we are fractals of God; we are a part of it, not separate. You do not need someone else to speak to God for you, speak to God yourself. That there is no fiery damnation for all of eternity. It is time to remove the fear. Follow the spiritual journey that makes you feel the happiest and the most fulfilled, then you will know you are on the right track.

Sending love and light!!

THE NEGATIVE
FRIENDSHIP FREQUENCY

Today's lesson of the day is about creating better boundaries with friends whose frequency is much lower than yours. You have worked very hard to raise your frequency. You have had experiences that began your spiritual journey, and now you are finding what used to serve you is no longer. Your friends have not changed – *you* have. You are now able to feel that shift within your mind and body.

You used to be such a social person, which is why you and your friends connected. Drinking and partying into the night was the norm. But ever since you have rediscovered yourself, you are feeling increasingly distant from the group. The friend group continues to be how they have always been, but you feel almost like a stranger in a strange land. And it continues feeling stranger and stranger.

They speak of the same issues that they never seem to learn from while you continue to grow from your own experiences. But now you feel badly about how you are feeling. You are afraid of losing your core group of friends, so you deal with it. Having a spiritual awakening can be difficult at times because you begin to understand the world better than you did before, and that makes you look at things differently.

You feel like you are the parent surrounded by children rather than friends, and it is beginning to weigh heavily on you. It is time to create boundaries. If it is not the right time to distance yourself from them, decline invitations when you are not up for it, remove yourself during toxic conversations, and never insert yourself into a situation that makes you uncomfortable. If they guilt trip you, or make you feel badly about your boundaries, you know where you stand.

Sending love and light!!

EMPLOYMENT TRAUMA

Today's lesson of the day is that you have a new job opportunity coming your way either now or soon, but you are beginning to allow trauma from past jobs to creep into your mind. You have been through one or more negative job experiences in your life, and you have dealt with toxic work environments involving co-workers and bosses. In the past, those people have made you second guess yourself, second guess your purpose, second guess everything.

Your past work environments have felt very similar to a middle school. Where people of power are afraid of your capabilities, so to keep you at bay, they made you feel less than in any way they could. There came a time when you even started to believe their lies for a moment. You thought, "Perhaps all of them were right." That maybe they knew you better than you knew yourself.

But that is farthest from the truth. You know yourself better than anyone could ever know you. You know how strong you are, how passionate you are, how creative. That type of energy terrifies those who could only wish they had your power. This is the time to step into your power now. Know your self-worth and use what you have learned for your next chapter. To shine even brighter than before.

In all actuality, it is not others who dim our light, it is *us* who believe the negative things others say that dims the light within us. So, rather than being fearful going into this new job, take what you have learned from your past toxic job experiences and harness that power to turn this new experience into something beautiful and positive; see the wonderful possibilities ahead. You are no longer the person you were before. You are even stronger! Trust.

Sending love and light!!

THE USE OF YOUR WISDOM

Today's lesson of the day is that you have a life decision to make, and you will need to use all your life experience and what you have learned to decide. Knowledge is power, and although you have had hard times in your life, they were always going to happen for a reason. Past choices that may or may not have worked out were to teach you and guide you into a certain direction. We may not consciously know what that direction is, but we are being led there.

Everything you have gone through was to help you prepare for this very moment. So, look at your choices with more experienced eyes now. What did you learn before that can help your decision? When making decisions, do so without fear, but with possibility, curiosity, and excitement. Listen to your heart and your gut feelings as they work together. Where are you being pulled?

Journal as well if it helps to write things down for more clarity. Write on every choice you have in front of you. How do you feel about each choice? What are you feeling in your body? What type of visceral response are you getting from each choice? Why do you think you are getting those feelings? Why do you feel you are being pulled towards one option than another?

The most important piece to remember, is to remove all fear, stress, and doubt from your decision. Fear keeps us away from our true purpose. It is an illusion created by our pasts and by societal beliefs. With fear removed, you will be limitless. Lead with love and gratitude, and you will be on your way to something beautiful! Trust and believe!

Sending love and light!!

RECOVERY FROM SURGERY
OR ILLNESS

Today's lesson of the day is to allow yourself to recover from a surgery or illness, and not to rush the process. Your body has been through a lot, and has caused you a lot of pain recently as you have overcome this unfortunate event. But recovery from such things takes time. In a world that is always fast moving, we now need to learn how to slow things down and be still. There is healing in the stillness.

Listen to your body. What is it telling you? Patience is the key. If you leap too soon, before you are ready to fly, you may end up harming yourself further. Healing in all forms is a process. This does not mean to stop your physical therapy or other forms of rehabilitation. On the contrary, that is very important. This means to honor your body when it needs to rest. Why are we so impatient during this process?

Because our souls do not need the rest, our physical bodies do. Our souls are like electricity to a machine; when the machine breaks down or needs repairs, electricity flowing through it is still strong and ready to go. Electricity does not need rest, but machines do. They can become worn out or overheated or damaged. It makes complete sense after our bodies need the rest to heal that our souls just want to keep going.

This is why you get so frustrated during this process that you want to get up and get back to your life at full speed. But these machines are currently a part of us now, and we must preserve them as best we can so that we can fulfill our missions here. So, take the time to recover. Find that stillness and feel the healing within it. Know that you will be back to the hustle and grind soon enough. Patience.

Sending love and light!!

COMMITMENT

Today's lesson of the day is about your current relationship and whether it is time to fully commit to them or let them go. Are you committed to this person or are you having second thoughts? You have been with them for quite some time, and you have been teetering between being unsure if you should commit fully to this person or if you are just not ready for the relationship.

If you are not fully sure by now, there must be a reason. You know the other person involved is all in, but you are still uncertain. The time to ask yourself, why you are unsure, is now. Do you feel you are settling? Is it because you have trust issues from the past, so you are hesitant to take those walls down? Are you only with the person because you do not want to be alone? Are the two of you so different that you cannot relate to each other? Are looks or the physical the only thing keeping you around?

There is always a "why." When you look at your relationship from the beginning, what was the big attraction in the first place? Has that original connection fizzled out over time or was it ever there? There are always reasons we begin to second guess ourselves. The reason we are feeling unsure is because our intuition or gut instinct is giving us those signs that something does not feel right or that something feels off.

Making connections is not easy, but is that a reason to settle for someone you truly do not click with? It is time to get to the bottom of how you are feeling, and if it is fear that is stopping you from committing, where is that fear coming from? What is the root cause? You have some work to do within right now, and once you have that clarity, you will know the right thing to do.

Sending love and light!!

FREEDOM FROM THE MENTAL PRISON

Today's lesson of the day is about how you were stuck in a mental prison where you doubted yourself for so long, but you are finally free. Through self-doubt you have been sabotaging yourself for years by not believing in yourself, instead listening to what others believed about you. Since you were younger, you slowly built those prison walls around you that have kept you stuck and unable to see the truth.

But now you know. You are breaking the walls down and clearing a new path for yourself. This is a triumphant moment for you. You were meant to go through everything you did to get to this incredible moment of enlightenment and empowerment. Many times, we must go through phases of doubt so we can understand and celebrate when we come out of it and see the truth.

You now see the beauty within you, and you feel like the world is opening to you after it felt so closed off before. The question is, what are you going to do with your newfound wisdom and power? You are limitless, but only if you believe that to be true. You have removed the blindfold, and you can see more clearly than you ever have before. You also see that the only thing that has been holding you back, is you.

Had you looked forward without the blindfold, you would have seen that the prison cell you created never had a door. It was open all along. So, now it is time to walk out of your own prison cell freely, with hope and possibility. Whenever you begin to doubt yourself again, remember what you have been through before and that will quickly remind you of your inner truth. Nothing is going to hold you back again.

Sending love and light!!

CLOSING THOUGHTS FROM YOUR FUTURE SELF

Dearest One,

I am writing to you from a place you have not yet seen, but that already lives within you. I want you to know that every step you have taken — even the ones that felt like mistakes — has been perfect. You have never once been off your path. Each choice, each joy, each heartbreak was the exact thread needed to weave the life you are now stepping into.

You have feared being too much, or not enough. You have wondered if your voice matters, if your presence makes a difference. I can tell you now with certainty: it does. You are more loved than you realize, and you are never alone. Your guides, your soul family, and your future self — me — have walked beside you through it all.

Trust that what you are building now is the foundation of a life that feels free, expansive, and deeply aligned with your soul. The doubts and heaviness you carry will not last forever. They are temporary clouds moving across an eternal sky that is you.

So, breathe. Lift your chin. Continue to walk forward with courage and curiosity. Love is waiting for you in places you cannot yet imagine. The best of your story has not even begun.

When you need strength, remember this: you have already made it. You are already whole. The journey is not about becoming; it is about remembering who you have always been.

And I promise you — you are magnificent.

With infinite love,

Your Future Self

CONTINUE YOUR JOURNEY

Thank you for walking with me through these divine lessons. Remember, your soul's path is ever-unfolding, and you are never alone on the journey.

If you feel called to go deeper, I invite you to visit my website:

www.GetKevInsight.com

There you'll find information about me, my readings and guidance, and updates on new books. May this be the beginning of an even greater unfolding in your life.

With love and light,

Kevin Wiczer

www.ingramcontent.com/pod-product-compliance
Lightning Source LLC
Chambersburg PA
CBHW021210130626
46554CB00004B/1161